HOWARD BRENTON

Howard Brenton was born in Portsmouth in 1942. His many plays include *Christie in Love* (Portable Theatre, 1969); *Revenge* (Theatre Upstairs, 1969); *Magnificence* (Royal Court Theatre, 1973); *The Churchill Play* (Nottingham Playhouse, 1974, and twice revived by the RSC, 1978 and 1988); *Bloody Poetry* (Foco Novo, 1984, and Royal Court Theatre, 1987); *Weapons of Happiness* (National Theatre, Evening Standard Award, 1976); *Epsom Downs* (Joint Stock Theatre, 1977); *Sore Throats* (RSC, 1978); *The Romans in Britain* (National Theatre, 1980, revived at the Crucible Theatre, Sheffield, 2006); *Thirteenth Night* (RSC, 1981); *The Genius* (1983), *Greenland* (1988) and *Berlin Bertie* (1992), all presented by the Royal Court; *Kit's Play* (RADA Jerwood Theatre, 2000); *Paul* (National Theatre, 2005); *In Extremis* (Shakespeare's Globe, 2006 and 2007); *Never So Good* (National Theatre, 2008); *The Ragged Trousered Philanthropists* adapted from the novel by Robert Tressell (Liverpool Everyman and Chichester Festival Theatre, 2010); *Anne Boleyn* (Shakespeare's Globe, 2010 and 2011); *55 Days* (Hampstead Theatre, 2012); *#aiww: The Arrest of Ai Weiwei* (Hampstead Theatre, 2013); *The Guffin* (NT Connections, 2013) and *Drawing the Line* (Hampstead Theatre, 2013).

Collaborations with other writers include *Brassneck* (with David Hare, Nottingham Playhouse, 1972); *Pravda* (with David Hare, National Theatre, Evening Standard Award, 1985) and *Moscow Gold* (with Tariq Ali, RSC, 1990).

Versions of classics include *The Life of Galileo* (1980) and *Danton's Death* (1982) both for the National Theatre, Goethe's *Faust* (1995/6) for the RSC, a new version of *Danton's Death* for the National Theatre (2010) and *Dances of Death* (Gate Theatre, 2013).

He wrote thirteen episodes of the BBC1 drama series *Spooks* (2001–05, BAFTA Best Drama Series, 2003).

Other Titles from Nick Hern Books

Howard Brenton

DOCTOR SCROGGY'S WAR

NICK HERN BOOKS

London

www.nickhernbooks.co.uk

A Nick Hern Book

Doctor Scroggy's War first published in Great Britain as a paperback original in 2014 by Nick Hern Books Limited, The Glasshouse, 49a Goldhawk Road, London W12 8QP

Doctor Scroggy's War copyright © 2014 Howard Brenton

Howard Brenton has asserted his right to be identified as the author of this work

Cover image: Tin mask from the Gillies Archive, photographed by Dr Andrew Bamji

Designed and typeset by Nick Hern Books, London
Printed in the UK by Mimeo Ltd, Huntingdon, Cambridgeshire PE29 6XX

A CIP catalogue record for this book is available from the British Library

ISBN 978 1 84842 421 0

Woodland
CARBON
www.woodlandcarbon.co.uk
NICK HERN BOOKS
Printed on Carbon Captured paper

Doctor Scroggy's War was first performed at Shakespeare's Globe, London, on 12 September 2014, with the following cast:

THE HON. PENELOPE WEDGEWOOD	Catherine Bailey
FIELD MARSHAL SIR DOUGLAS HAIG	Sam Cox
MR TWIGG	Patrick Driver
JACK TWIGG	Will Featherstone
HAROLD GILLIES	James Garnon
TILLY HOPE	Daisy Hughes
LORD RALPH DULWICH	Joe Jameson
CORPORAL CLANCY/ LIEUTENANT JONES	Tom Kanji
SIR WILLIAM ARBUTHNOT-LANE	Christopher Logan
CORPORAL FERGAL O'HANNAGAN	William Mannering
MEGAN JONES	Holly Morgan
CATHERINE BLACK	Rhiannon Oliver
LIEUTENANT MACHAN/ PRIVATE EDWARDS	Keith Ramsay
FIELD MARSHAL SIR JOHN FRENCH	Paul Rider
MRS TWIGG/QUEEN MARY	Katy Stephens
MARSHAL JOFFRE/ LIEUTENANT HARDY	Dickon Tyrrell

Director	John Dove
Designer	Michael Taylor
Composer	Bill Lyons
Choreographer	Sian Williams
Globe Associate – Movement	Glynn Macdonald
Voice and Dialect Coach	Martin McKellan
Fight Director	Terry King
Assistant Director	Josh Roche
Costume Supervisor	Hilary Lewis

Acknowledgements

Many thanks to Dr Andrew Bamji FRCP, the Gillies Archivist at the British Association of Plastic, Reconstructive and Aesthetic Surgeons, for his tireless advice on medical matters and his insights into Gillies' work and character. I am also indebted to the writer and cultural researcher George Simmers for his advice on military matters and the many discussions we had about the mores of the time. The artistic licence taken and any howlers that may still lie undetected are entirely my responsibility.

H.B.

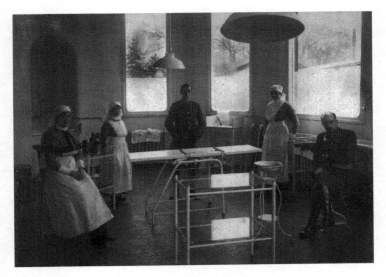

Queen's Hospital staff in the Plastic Theatre, autumn 1917. Harold Gillies is seated on the right; the officer standing is his first anaesthetist, Captain Rubens Wade.

Characters

HAROLD GILLIES, *thirty-three*
MEGAN JONES ⎫ *VAD nurses*
TILLY HOPE ⎭
CATHERINE BLACK, *nursing sister*
SIR WILLIAM ARBUTHNOT LANE
JACK TWIGG, *twenty-two*
MR ROY TWIGG
MRS RACHAEL TWIGG
LORD RALPH DULWICH, *twenty-five*
THE HON. PENELOPE WEDGEWOOD
FIELD MARSHAL SIR JOHN FRENCH
FIELD MARSHAL SIR DOUGLAS HAIG
MARSHAL JOSEPH JOFFRE
CORPORAL FERGAL O'HANNAGAN
CORPORAL CLANCY
HER MAJESTY QUEEN MARY

MAJOR DOMO
LIEUTENANT MACHAN (*only screaming*)
GOLD CLUB MEMBER
WOOZY WOMAN AT THE RITZ
REJECTED MAN AT THE RITZ
A BRIGADIER AT GHQ
TWO STRETCHER-BEARERS
PRIVATE EDWARDS
LIEUTENANTS HARDY *and* JONES, *patients at Sidcup*

And DANCERS *and* WAITERS AT THE RITZ, BRITISH AND
FRENCH HIGH-RANKING OFFICERS, PRIVATES *in the
trench*, NURSES

*This text went to press before the end of rehearsals and so may
differ slightly from the play as performed.*

ACT ONE

Scene One

Aldershot 1915. A golf course.

HAROLD GILLIES – *tall, fit, bald, in the uniform of an army major – is on a tee. He has a large driver club in one hand and an empty beer bottle in the other. His large, battered doctor's bag is a distance away.*

GILLIES (*aside*). Play golf. Good for my arm, stiff elbow. I got the elbow when I was eleven, got its stiffness, I mean. I saw one of my aunts on the lavatory, was terrified, fled and fell downstairs. No ill effects, don't know about the aunt. Now, driving off.

He puts the beer bottle down.

Theory is – ball elevation. Hit the golf ball at a greater height, catching the full upward force of the swing of the club. And, after many experiments, I find the perfect height for the ball is: top of a beer bottle.

He takes a golf ball from his pocket and puts the ball on the neck of the beer bottle. He adopts a driving position to one side of the beer bottle and demonstrates in slow motion.

See, the club head swings through... rises, impact and... wallop! Right.

He squares up to hit the ball.

Fore!

He is about to hit the ball. Enter a handlebar-moustached MEMBER OF THE SIDCUP GOLF CLUB COMMITTEE. *He is incensed.*

MEMBER. Gillies, in God's name, glass all over the tees!

GILLIES. Galileo understood.

MEMBER. Galla-who?

GILLIES. He wasn't all down a telescope.

MEMBER. What in hell's name are you talking about?

GILLIES. Galileo Galilei, father of mechanics as well as astronomer, in his great work, the *Discorsi*, calculated the transfer of energy from one object to another, as in head of golf club to golf ball.

Squares up again.

MEMBER. There have been complaints! It's dangerous and damn inconsiderate!

GILLIES. Can't improve a golf swing without breaking eggs.

MEMBER. You're going to drive golf balls off eggs?

GILLIES. Metaphor, old man. As in omelettes. Fore!

He hits the golf ball into the auditorium. The beer bottle shatters. [NB: the ball is a ping-pong ball, the bottle made of sugar glass?] They stare out into the auditorium.

MEMBER (*stunned*). Smithers.

GILLIES. What do you think, dear heart? Two hundred and thirty-five, forty yards?

MEMBER. No, no, can't be having this, Gillies! This... experimenting! It's not golf, it's not... natural!

As they talk, CATHERINE BLACK, *a hospital sister in uniform, rides on to the stage on a bicycle and dismounts.*

CATHERINE. Major Gillies!

GILLIES. Nothing more natural than human experimentation. Disaster though it can be.

MEMBER. As committee chairman, it is my duty to warn you. Any more glass on the tees and you will be barred.

CATHERINE. Major Gillies. It's the Lieutenant.

MEMBER. Do I make myself clear?

GILLIES *stares at him as if he does not know who he is, then turns back to* CATHERINE. *Then with rapid movement he collects his bag.*

GILLIES. Hop me on, sister.

GILLIES *climbs onto the bike with her. She pedals them away.*

MEMBER. Gillies... Look, hold on... Gillies!

GILLIES. Glass! Mind the tyres!

GILLIES *and* CATHERINE *exit on the bicycle.*

MEMBER (*aside*). They say he's brilliant. But the last thing a golf club needs on the fairway is a bloody genius. I mean, there is a war on.

He exits.

Scene Two

Two VAD nurses – MEGAN JONES, *Welsh, and* TILLY HOPE, *posh – enter, pulling on a hospital bed at speed. The* LIEUTENANT *is lying on it. His face is covered with a dressing saturated in blood. He is crying out, a heart-rending, strangulated, repeated cry.*

LIEUTENANT. Ah! Ah! Ah!

Then he is silent. His body arches in pain.

MEGAN. Lieutenant!

TILLY. Robert!

MEGAN. Lieutenant!

TILLY. Oxygen...

MEGAN. Can't, got no face has he, has he, no face, no face...

TILLY. Robert, please, oh, Robert...

They freeze. The LIEUTENANT *is still.*

GILLIES *enters running, pulling on a surgical gown.*
CATHERINE *enters after him.*

GILLIES (*to the* ANNIE). How long?

TILLY. Mask for the oxygen, got no face...

CATHERINE. Pull yourself together, girl! How long has it been?

MEGAN. Half a minute...

GILLIES. Bobby old thing, I want no nonsense here!

He leaps on the bed and is astride the LIEUTENANT.

CATHERINE. What...

GILLIES. Closed cardiac massage, dearie. Tad controversial but
   so is death.

The NURSES *step back.* GILLIES *pumps the*
LIEUTENANT'*s chest many times.*

Bobby!... Not... in... this... hospital...

No reaction. He stops. He gets off the bed, exhausted.

CATHERINE. Major Gillies...

GILLIES. Imagine opening the chest, and holding the heart in
   your hand... and giving direct cardiac massage, a rhythmic
   squeeze... wouldn't that be something, my dears, wouldn't
   that be... a lovely thing. (*A beat.*) Time?

CATHERINE *looks at a watch pinned to her.*

CATHERINE. 3.22 p.m.

GILLIES. Record it.

CATHERINE. Yes, Major.

GILLIES *walks away from the bed. His gown is smeared
   with blood.*

(*To* TILLY *and* MEGAN, *meaning the body.*) Nurses, lay
   him out.

MEGAN. I can't...

TILLY. No, I...

CATHERINE (*irritated*). Oh, do toughen up, girls. Never mind, I'll do for him. Now...

A gesture: take him away.

The NURSES *exit, pulling the bed and the* LIEUTENANT's *body with them.*

These VAD girls, why do they volunteer, when they are so squeamish?

GILLIES. They de-squeam soon enough.

GILLIES *takes off his gown and throws it down in a fury. He stares at it.*

What? (*A beat.*) Say what you are going to say. (*A beat.*) Catherine! (*A beat.*) Why haven't you said it yet?

CATHERINE. Giles, it's not your bloody fault!

Both still.

Sorry, sir, speaking out of hand.

GILLIES. No, no, Catherine, I am out of hand. But, yes, fault line there is and the fault is mine!

CATHERINE. Lieutenant Machan wanted the operation.

He makes delicate movements with his hand in front of his face, as if cutting with a scalpel, then he puts his hand to his face. Then looks up.

GILLIES. Young-buck airman, beautiful chap. You know they don't tell their superiors they fly back from France at weekends, for parties? Great boys. Of course he wanted the damn operation! He had no face!

CATHERINE. He threatened to do away with himself.

GILLIES. Jolly good, I did the job for him.

CATHERINE. His face was burnt away, he'd lost an eye, he was all but blinded in the other.

GILLIES. I should have waited. But I did not. Because of...
pity. Pity is bad in a surgeon. It kills.

And SIR WILLIAM ARBUTHNOT LANE *enters.*

ARBUTHNOT LANE. Been slaughtering patients, Giles?

GILLIES. Something like.

CATHERINE. Colonel, sir, I had no idea...

ARBUTHNOT LANE. Don't worry, sister. This is not a sudden
inspection from on high. Absolutely fruitless exercise with
Major Gillies anyway.

He smiles.

CATHERINE (*to* GILLIES). I must lay out...

GILLIES. Yes.

CATHERINE. Please excuse me, sir.

ARBUTHNOT LANE. Of course, sister.

Exit CATHERINE.

An army staff nurse, laying out a deceased?

GILLIES. She took pity on the VADs.

ARBUTHNOT LANE. I wonder about these volunteer girls,
what the hell they expect.

GILLIES. Can't be hard on 'em. I remember the shock of my
first corpse. Couldn't move, couldn't breathe.

ARBUTHNOT LANE. Who was he?

GILLIES. Uncle of mine. Found him dead at Christmas.
Knocked over the tree. Trauma of the aorta. Didn't know
what it was then, of course, I was ten.

ARBUTHNOT LANE. No, I meant who was the young man...

GILLIES. Lieutenant, Royal Flying Corps. Actually he wasn't
injured in France, he crashed in training. Didn't even get the
chance to party across the channel.

ARBUTHNOT LANE. Crashes in training, yes. Too many.

GILLIES. There should be ambulances on every airfield.

ARBUTHNOT LANE. I'll talk to the Royal Flying Corps.

GILLIES. We pick up the pieces. The lumps. I'm talking flesh.

ARBUTHNOT LANE. That's what we're here to do. (*A hesitation*.) Was he burnt?

GILLIES. Way, way beyond.

ARBUTHNOT LANE. What did you do?

GILLIES. Attempted to replace the whole skin of the face by a chest flap.

ARBUTHNOT LANE. You've had brilliant success with chest flaps.

GILLIES makes hand movements in front of his face again, as if he is imagining an operation.

GILLIES. But by being slow, letting things heal, quarter of the face, then another quarter. I told him, wait, let nature heal, wait! But the poor boy begged me, do it all at once, give me my face. And the nursing staff warned me, he was threatening to kill himself.

ARBUTHNOT LANE. Then you had no choice.

GILLIES. There is always a choice. I made the wrong one. The flap failed, gangrene, then infection and the infection got to his heart.

ARBUTHNOT LANE. Giles…

GILLIES. I will never let that happen again. I will wait. Never do today what can be honourably put off to tomorrow. (*A beat*.) Yes.

He walks around quickly, repeating the scalpel-like gestures, mouthing words to himself.

ARBUTHNOT LANE *is about to intervene but* GILLIES *stops.*

So, what from the beasts on high?

ARBUTHNOT LANE. The War Office say you can have more beds, here at Aldershot.

GILLIES. But there's only one ward. I need a whole hospital. William, don't they know what's coming? What trench war means? Tommy pops his head up to have a peep at the Kaiser, bang! There will be thousands of poor boys with facial injuries beyond imagining.

ARBUTHNOT LANE. The War Office is going to order the distribution of tin hats...

GILLIES (*whirling around*). Where's Scroggy?

ARBUTHNOT LANE. Who?

GILLIES. I mean my bag. My bag. Ah there you are.

He goes to his bag he takes out a piece of rusted, jagged metal and a piece of flint.

Souvenirs from my time in France. This... (*The metal fragment.*) from the casing of a shell fired from a German 150 millimetre howitzer. Imagine the moment! It's hot, it's spinning, jagged, covered with mud and microbes and it... takes half your jaw your ear and an eye, half your face...

He wipes it past ARBUTHNOT LANE's face, who recoils. He holds up the flint.

And flints, chalky ground, shells hit and thousands of flints are in the air, spinning, whizz! There's your nose gone, oh and throw in your upper teeth and palate, upper jawbone... Tin bloody hats?

He throws the piece of metal and the flint back in the bag.

If the War Office brings in tin bloody hats, know what they'll mean?

ARBUTHNOT LANE. Saved lives...

GILLIES. But what lives? What kind of lives? Give 'em tin hats and boys will survive with smashed faces, when they would have died before.

He is dead still, staring down at his opened bag.

A silence.

ARBUTHNOT LANE *is about to speak. Then* GILLIES *snaps out of it.*

Lunch?

ARBUTHNOT LANE. Very much so...

GILLIES. Give me a moment, will you, dear heart?

ARBUTHNOT LANE (*hesitates for a moment*). Giles, of course. (*Exits.*)

GILLIES *looks down at the bag. Then he pulls it open violently and glares down into it.*

GILLIES. What you say?

Wags his finger at the bag. Then he straightens.

Yes. Right question, Scroggy. How many more young men will I fail?

A moment. Then he snaps the bag shut and exits quickly as...

Scene Three

JACK TWIGG *enters. He is in the uniform of a lieutenant of the London Regiment. He looks about him.*

JACK (*London accent*). Mum? Dad?

LORD RALPH DULWICH *enters. He is in the uniform of a lieutenant. He keeps his distance.*

RALPH (*aside. Upper-class accent*). I say, God what. A whiff out of Old Father Thames' backside round here. Are there people who actually work in this stink?

Enter MR ROY TWIGG, JACK*'s father. He wears a large dark-green apron. He is pulling a small cart loaded with* *ship's supplies. He is a small, compact, tough-looking man but when he speaks his manner is warm.*

JACK. Dad…

MR TWIGG. Old boy, what you been and done?

JACK. What do you mean?

MR TWIGG. Them togs.

JACK. It's a uniform, Dad.

MR TWIGG. I can see that, I can see that very well!

JACK. It's of the London Irish Rifles.

MR TWIGG. I don't care what it's of, what is it doing on you?

JACK. I'm a lieutenant.

A pause.

MR TWIGG. And what am I?

JACK. Dad, don't fly off the handle…

MR TWIGG. I'll do what I like with my handle! Just tell me, what am I?

JACK. Dad…

MR TWIGG. Rooted, that's what I am! Rooted to the spot! London Irish? You in't Irish!

JACK. Most of us in the regiment aren't.

RALPH *steps forward.*

RALPH. It's a jolly fashionable outfit, Mr Twigg, sir. Chaps are giving hen's teeth to get in.

MR TWIGG. And what may you be?

JACK. Dad, this is my friend, Lord Dulwich…

MR TWIGG. Lord?

RALPH. I'm delighted to make your acquaintance. Jack has spoken so very warmly about you.

MR TWIGG. Has he now. (*A moment. But he shakes* RALPH's *hand.*) Well. Please don't think me rude, my lordship...

RALPH. Ralph...

MR TWIGG. My Ralphship... I've got to ask you, man to man, as men we are: did you put him up to it?

RALPH. Sir, I think it was your son's sense of duty 'put him up to it'.

MR TWIGG. Do you have the slightest twinkling of a noddle of a notion of what it takes for a lad from round here to get to Oxford? Son of a ship's chandler and all?

JACK. We decided to join together, Dad.

MR TWIGG. All that book-bashing, all that examining, that dream of them dreaming spires: your future, Jack! What it could mean, them lovely college walls, all yellowy, the green of that quad, never seen anything like it, so... smooth... and gentlemen walking round it in the sunshine, in gowns... and you one of 'em! Now you're chucking all that away?

JACK. There's nothing to chuck, Dad. There are tents all over the quad, the army's taking over the college. And we're all signing up. It's a great thing.

MR TWIGG. Not saying it ain't a great thing. I just wish it weren't a thing at all.

JACK. Can't wish away the Hun, Dad! He raped Belgium.

MRS RACHAEL TWIGG *has entered. She catches sight of* JACK *and staggers.*

MRS TWIGG. Oh my giddy aunt, he's gone and signed up.

JACK. Hello, Mum.

MRS TWIGG. Look at you! Spit 'n' polish!

JACK. Mum, this is my friend Ralph.

MRS TWIGG. Hello, Mr Ralph, I'm sure.

RALPH. I'm delighted to make your acquaintance, Mrs Twigg.

MRS TWIGG. Well, we're as you find us. So our Jack's talked you into the army too, has he?

RALPH. Yes, it was Jack's idea.

MRS TWIGG. He were always army-mad, even when he was a kiddie. He did the Battle of Waterloo on the parlour carpet.

MR TWIGG. Them bloody tin soldiers! They were what started it! Worse bloody birthday present ever!

They stare at him. Embarrassment. A pause.

MRS TWIGG. Roy!

MR TWIGG. I'm sorry, I... The shock of it, it's turned me inside out that's all. I'm proud, course I'm proud. My boy, doing the right thing. King and country and saving Belgium, poor little thing.

MRS TWIGG. Ralph, is it? Well, Ralphy...

MR TWIGG (*sotto*). Rachael, he's a lord.

MRS TWIGG. Well, they have 'em at Oxford don't they, that's why we wanted Jack to go there! Be amongst lords! Turn into one himself!

Roars with laughter. Curtseys to RALPH.

MR TWIGG. Rachael, please, don't get jolly. Last thing we need is you jolly.

MRS TWIGG. Oooh, sorry, your lordship, but a bit of glorious and I get carried away. What I was going to say was let's have tea.

RALPH. Tea...

JACK (*to* RALPH). Supper.

RALPH. Mrs Twigg, that is very kind of you but unfortunately...

JACK (*interrupting*). We've been invited to a reception. At The Ritz.

It's very important. It's being given by Sir John French.

MR TWIGG. Sir John French? Field Marshal Sir John French? But he's…

RALPH. Commander-in-Chief, yes.

JACK. Ralph's got me in.

RALPH. Family thing. My father was with Sir John at Elandslaagte.

MR TWIGG. Eland-what…

JACK. Battle of Elandslaagte, Dad. South Africa, Boer War.

RALPH. My father was Sir John's aide-de-camp.

MR TWIGG. Oh. Very nice.

JACK. Ralph is going to be on Sir John's staff.

MR TWIGG. Nicer.

JACK. An intelligence officer.

MR TWIGG. Yes? And what do they do?

RALPH. Well… Be intelligent. It's just about all arranged.

JACK. So it's very important we go. And I'm afraid we can't stay to tea. But I'll be back tonight, if that's all right…

MRS TWIGG. Course it's all right, my lovely.

MR TWIGG. When do you go to France?

JACK. Tomorrow morning. Six o'clock. Victoria Station.

They are stunned.

We've done the basic training and we're going to do more in Normandy.

MR TWIGG. Six in the morning.

JACK. But I will see you tonight.

MRS TWIGG. Well, I'll get your bed nice and aired.

Sticky.

JACK. Well…

RALPH. Mr and Mrs Twigg, it's been a pleasure to meet you.

He kisses her hand.

MRS TWIGG. Lordy, my lord...

RALPH. Ralph.

MRS TWIGG. Yes please.

JACK. See you tonight.

MRS TWIGG. Have a splendourifically wonderful time.

JACK. 'Splendourifically wonderful' it will be, Mum.

They hug each other.

MRS TWIGG. I'm so proud.

RALPH (*aside*). Ha! Poor old Jack, eh? I had no idea! Bank of the Thames? Damn little mudlark! Won't let on though, don't want him ribbed in the mess, decent little fellow. Rather touched he wanted to show me off. And royally shown off have I been. Now we can go and get absolutely rotted.

MRS TWIGG. *Au revoir!*

JACK *and* RALPH *exit cheerfully, waving. The* TWIGGS *wave back and are alone.*

Well. Never and a day.

MR TWIGG. I should say.

A pause.

MRS TWIGG. You are proud too, ain't you, Roy?

MR TWIGG. Course I am. Now the shock is over.

MRS TWIGG. France in the morning. He'll need to take some food that won't go off, what do you think, my dry-cured mutton?

MR TWIGG. Your pride and joy. Let's have our tea, shall we?

MRS TWIGG. Supper!

MR TWIGG. Yes, yes.

MRS TWIGG. He will be all right, won't he.

MR TWIGG. Your mutton under his belt, he'll go at the Hun hell for leather.

MRS TWIGG. I just don't want him to hurt his lovely eyes.

Scene Four

Dancing couples sweep onto the stage. All the men are in uniform. The women are beautifully dressed.

Then JACK and RALPH walk on. They take glasses of champagne from a WAITER. JACK is fazed.

JACK. It's a party.

RALPH. Of course it's a party. What did you think it would be?

MAJOR DOMO. The Honourable Penelope Wedgewood.

Enter the HON. PENELOPE WEDGEWOOD. She too has a glass of champagne in her hand. She looks around.

JACK. Well, it's with the Commander-in-Chief. I thought it would be... serious. Battle tactics.

PENELOPE approaches RALPH and JACK.

RALPH. Johnny French's parties are battles.

PENELOPE (*to* RALPH). Oh look, a very bad man.

RALPH. Hello, Penny.

PENELOPE. And who is this you are corrupting?

JACK. I...

RALPH. This is Lieutenant Jack Twigg and he is a friend of mine and you are to leave him alone. Jack, this is the Honourable Penelope Wedgewood.

JACK. I'm very pleased to meet you, Miss Wedgewood.

PENELOPE (*looks at him for a moment*). Oh. Good. I am leaving you alone.

JACK. Thank God for that! Ha!

They stare at him.

I mean... I... Er... (*Aside.*) I mean oh God she's so beautiful and oh God if she looks at me again I'll make a fool of myself.

PENELOPE (*to* RALPH). Ralphy, waft me away!

RALPH. 'Scuse us, old man.

They put their glasses onto the WAITER*'s tray and swirl into the dance as...*

PENELOPE. Where did you find *him*?

RALPH. A stray from Oxford.

PENELOPE. Does look a bit of a dog.

JACK *has heard this. He presses his knees together.*

JACK (*aside*). Dog. Well. That's me in my place. I know I'll never be one of them. Ralph's all right, he's fun, but when I'm with toffs I feel... thin, weedy, like I'm not really... here. That I'm pressing my knees together. (*Looks down.*) Oh God I am pressing my knees together! This is what the English class system does to you. (*Straightens his legs.*) But what really scares me about the toffs is: do they know how to fight the war? Because I do, I know I do.

MAJOR DOMO. Field Marshal Sir John French.

Enter FIELD MARSHAL SIR JOHN FRENCH. *The dancers stop at once. The men salute, the women applaud enthusiastically. They surround him.*

PENELOPE. Johnny darling.

FRENCH. Penny, my dear, you look top-hole. Thoroughly delicious and eatable.

PENELOPE. Thank you very much, Field Marshal.

RALPH. Good evening, sir.

FRENCH (*a slightly myopic moment*). Ah. Dulwich's boy.

RALPH. Yes, sir.

FRENCH. Your father wanted me to do something for you. Am I doing something for you?

RALPH. Well, I, er...

FRENCH (*suddenly at* JACK). Lieutenant!

JACK (*startled*). Yes, Field Marshal!

FRENCH. White!

JACK. Sir?

FRENCH. White bubbles! What's all this damn white bubbly? Pink! Pink bubbles tonight!

JACK. I...

RALPH (*sotto*). Throw the damn drink away.

JACK flicks the drink away.

FRENCH. Good man!

Everyone looks at each other, then they throw their drinks away. The WAITER *distributes new glasses of champagne.*

The 1st London?

JACK. Yes, sir!

FRENCH. Good man! Coming to France?

JACK. Yes, sir!

FRENCH. Good man! (*To the* WAITER.) Maître! Glass!

The WAITER *hurries to pour pink champagne into* JACK's *glass.*

Good health!

ALL. Good health!

FRENCH. Right, young minds, bright and shiny, I envy you gentlemen, seeing the world as new. Does look all shiny, doesn't it?

RALPH. Yes, sir.

JACK.... Yes, sir.

FRENCH. So... (*To* RALPH.) *Arme blanche?* (*A beat.*) For or against?

RALPH. Sir?

FRENCH (*to* JACK). Lieutenant?

JACK. I believe in the lance.

FRENCH. Do you, by God!

JACK. As you did, sir, when you won the battle of Elandslaagte.

RALPH. Yes, the cavalryman's lance, I...

FRENCH (*to* RALPH). Let the man have his say! (*To* JACK.) So?

JACK. The lance is part of a cavalryman's being. Trench warfare won't go on for ever.

FRENCH. The modern school would have 'em done away with altogether. It's the age of the bullet not the lance. What do you say to that?

JACK. Cavalry are not infantry on horseback.

FRENCH. They are to High Command. Know better than your betters, huh?

He looks around.

Huh?

Laughter at JACK.

JACK. Take away the lance and it will destroy morale, sir. The cavalry are all about morale. The charge. It's always been that way.

RALPH. Yes, like the cavalry at the Battle of Agincourt.

FRENCH (*to* JACK). What's wrong with that?

JACK. There were no English cavalry at Agincourt.

FRENCH. Why not?

JACK. They'd eaten all the horses.

FRENCH. Ha! Clever little bugger, are you?

JACK. Yes, sir, I mean no, sir.

RALPH. But Wellington won Waterloo with infantry.

JACK. But he had cavalry. The Scots Greys. Engaged
Napoleon's lancers.

RALPH. But it was rifle fire from squares won the battle.

FRENCH. Truth is, Wellington was losing. What tipped it over
was Marshal Blücher's Prussians, arriving late. A cavalry
charge. Where, Twigg?

JACK. Napoleon's right flank.

FRENCH. Correct! Ironic, eh? Actually, the Battle of Waterloo
was won by the bloody Hun.

FRENCH *laughs*.

JACK. There will always be cavalry in war. They are immortal.

Has he spoken out of turn too much? FRENCH *is staring
at him.*

FRENCH. Until they're cut to bits. You two young blades have
never seen it, men cut down in a charge. But you will. The
beastliness of it, and the glory.

FRENCH *turns away then turns back.*

(*To* JACK.) Need a junior intelligence officer on my staff.
Up for it?

JACK. I, er… Yes, sir.

RALPH *is shocked.*

FRENCH. I'll bump you up to captain. Report to my HQ in Saint-Omer, immediately you are in France.

JACK. Yes, sir.

FRENCH. Field promotion on the floor of The Ritz ballroom. Bit of a first, eh? What? What?

Laughter all round.

Penelope my dear, may I have the honour?

PENELOPE (*low to* JACK). What a clever boy we are. (*To* FRENCH.) Delighted, Sir John.

Music.

FRENCH *and* PENELOPE *lead the whirling dancers away and they all exit but for* JACK *and* RALPH.

RALPH. You arse-licking little shit.

JACK. What?

RALPH. You weaselly, wheedling creep.

JACK. What? No...

RALPH. That was my place at HQ! That was for me! My father spoke to Sir John!

JACK. Well, didn't speak loud enough, did he!

RALPH. What did you say, creep?

JACK. It's not my fault, Ralph.

RALPH. Henry the bloody Fifth eating his horse, Waterloo? You swotted that up, just to arse lick.

JACK. The battles that made England great, they're part of us, we're soldiers...

RALPH. Real soldier's a gentleman, which you are not. You're a nothing, a back-stabber, a wheedler. You mentioned the old boy's battle deliberately, didn't you!

JACK. Elandslaagte was a classic cavalry charge...

RALPH. You sucked up. You're a lower-class brat, sucking up to your betters. A jumped-up Thames mudlark, that's you, Twigg.

JACK. Captain Twigg.

RALPH *stares at him then salutes and walks away.*

Ralph, I didn't mean to...

But RALPH *exits.* JACK *turns away to leave but* PENELOPE *enters.*

PENELOPE. So. You are the golden boy.

JACK. I don't know about that.

PENELOPE. I do.

JACK. Ah. Hum.

PENELOPE. What did you say?

JACK. Hum.

PENELOPE. How did you manage to get into the London Irish? Pretty eyes?

JACK. Hum... I...

PENELOPE. There something the matter with you?

JACK. Yes, I think there may be.

PENELOPE. So do I. You're different. Why is that?

JACK. It's because I'm made of mud.

PENELOPE. Mud?

JACK. Thames mud.

PENELOPE. So you're not an officer and a gentleman at all.

JACK. No.

A beat. She looks at him. Frowns then smiles.

PENELOPE. Well, whatever you are, the Field Marshal's very loyal to his men. A different story with women, but that's little jolly Johnny.

JACK. He's Commander-in-Chief! You can't call him that.

PENELOPE. But I do. Do you want to know what he calls me? No, you don't. Because you are shockable.

JACK. No, I'm not.

PENELOPE. Really? He calls me...

She leans into him, whispers into his ear then turns away.

JACK. Oh. My.

PENELOPE. Barrack-room stuff.

JACK. Oh my.

PENELOPE. I expect you call your women worse. (*Aside.*) I know, I'm a fool for cherry lips and a uniform. And he says he's made of mud, how can a girl resist? (*To* JACK.) The innocent ones always turn out to be brutes. Are you? A brute?

JACK. Look I'm really sorry, miss, I...

PENELOPE. Miss? (*Aside.*) Oh. Bolt from the blue! (*To* JACK.) Are you a virgin?

JACK. No, I'm a chap.

PENELOPE. I'm very sorry. Jack, isn't it? Sorry. (*But she giggles.*)

JACK. You thought I was a cad. Is that what you're saying?

PENELOPE. Well, most of you at Johnny's parties are absolutely bloody swines with peas for brains. But you're all heroes. You are a hero.

JACK. I haven't done anything yet!

PENELOPE. You will. (*A pause.*) When do you leave?

JACK. In the morning.

PENELOPE. So it's going to be like that then.

JACK. What is going to be like what?

PENELOPE *goes to him and kisses him. They embrace.*

I say.

PENELOPE. No, don't say a thing. (*Takes his hand*.) Come on.

JACK. I really don't know if...

PENELOPE. Don't worry, I've got a room.

JACK. In The Ritz?

PENELOPE. Daddy keeps a suite.

JACK (*aside*). Oh God, who is Daddy?

PENELOPE. If little Johnny French knocks on the door, no giggles. (*A beat*.) Yes?

JACK. Yes.

They hold hands and exit running.

Scene Five

A WOOZY COUPLE *enter. He is in uniform. They embrace. He says something in her ear. She pushes him away.*

REJECTED MAN. I say, I am going to France, y'know.

WOMAN. Not far enough for me.

REJECTED MAN. I mean, if a chap's going to give his life, a gal can give her y'know what...

She slaps his face and exits, running.

Damn unfair.

He exits. JACK *enters in his underwear. He is in a daze. He stumbles.*

PENELOPE *enters, in a long nightgown, smoking a cigarette in a holder and carrying a bottle of champagne with the fingertips of the other hand. She observes him.*

JACK (*aside*). Gosh. I mean... So that's what... Oh. I mean... Oh. (*Turns to* PENELOPE.) Marry me.

She looks at him. A pause.

PENELOPE. You've got half an hour.

JACK. Half an hour to marry you?

PENELOPE. To get to Victoria.

JACK. What? (*Looks at watch.*) Oh no.

PENELOPE. I'll pop you in a taxi.

JACK. Oh, Mum, Dad, I was going to go home!

PENELOPE. Too late, my hero.

JACK. Will you marry me?

PENELOPE. I could, I could not, who knows?

She laughs.

JACK. I do.

PENELOPE. Oh please. No one is innocent, it's silly to pretend.

JACK. I don't understand.

PENELOPE (*aside*). Oh God, I don't think he does, how long is he going to last?

She kisses him passionately then steps back.

Your breath's awful! I've got some toothpaste, swallow some and take the tube.

JACK. We have tins.

PENELOPE. What?

JACK. At home. We have tooth powder in tins.

PENELOPE. You really are an old-fashioned boy.

JACK. I want to marry you!

PENELOPE. No, you don't. Really, you don't. (*Takes his hand.*) Right, Captain Jack Twigg! Chop-chop! Trousers on and off to France!

They exit.

Scene Six

Enter MR TWIGG. *He is smoking a pipe. He paces.*

MR TWIGG (*aside*). Jack, old boy, my dear heart, what you thinking of?

Enter MRS TWIGG. *She has a basket covered by a cloth.*

MRS TWIGG. It's six o'clock. He'll be on the train and I got his food.

MR TWIGG. He'll be... you know.

MRS TWIGG. No, I don't know. Do I?

MR TWIGG. It's a big, posh hotel. And the army? It's a man's world. Sorry to be indelicate.

A moment.

MRS TWIGG. No, Jack's a good boy. He said he was coming home, 'fore he gets the train! Oh my good God. The Germans have got him.

MR TWIGG. He's nowhere near France yet, Rachael.

MRS TWIGG. But what about the spies?

MR TWIGG. What spies?

MRS TWIGG. All over London.

MR TWIGG. Who says there're spies?

MRS TWIGG. They say so.

MR TWIGG. Who is this they?

MRS TWIGG. They, people, British, English, us.

MR TWIGG. And do we? Say there're German spies all over London?

MRS TWIGG. What worries me is they've got into The Ritz.

MR TWIGG. How they done that, then?

MRS TWIGG. I don't know! Through the kitchens, or bathroom windows, or up through the drains, like rats... Germans! Out to kill young officers, or kidnap them. Yeah, that's what they're doing! They're snatching our boys and taking 'em in U-boats 'cross the North Sea...

MR TWIGG. I can't see how that is militarily advantageous.

MRS TWIGG. I'd believe anything of the Hun. Remember what they did in Belgium.

MR TWIGG. Yeah. Poor little Belgium.

MRS TWIGG. Bayonetting little babies.

MR TWIGG. Dearie dearie me, oh yes...

MRS TWIGG. And that nurse with her poor breasts cut off, nailed to a church door.

MR TWIGG. Dearie dearie.

MRS TWIGG. And Belgian nuns tied to the clappers of bells in their convent so when the bells were rung... blood rained down. And now the Hun's got our Jack!

MR TWIGG. The Hun's not, my dear, he's not.

For a moment she stares at him.

MRS TWIGG. They are true, in't they. The stories.

MR TWIGG. I...

MRS TWIGG. They got to be true. Nuns on bells. Belgian babies. Cos if they're not true, what's Jack risking his life for?

MR TWIGG. Course they're true. We know the Hun.

MRS TWIGG. Sorry of the wobbles.

MR TWIGG. It's a time of wobbles.

MRS TWIGG. No it's not. Cos we're going to come through.

MR TWIGG. Yes.

MRS TWIGG. Jack will come through.

MR TWIGG. Course he will, he loves his soldiering.

MRS TWIGG. I'll put this in the larder. Then we'll get on with our day.

MR TWIGG. Yes, my dear.

She exits.

MR TWIGG (*aside*). Our beautiful boy, yes. We made him. But what you going to do to him, England? What are you going to do?

He exits as...

Scene Seven

Enter JACK. He is smoking a cigarette. He carries a folded map.

The distant sound of long-range artillery.

JACK (*aside*). Plane trees in avenues along the roads. Sunlight and leaves. And there are girls in the fields, a harvest, they are bringing in a harvest. Where is the war? (*A beat.*) It's there. Just. You don't exactly hear the guns, they are in the back of your head. (*A beat.*) France. Saint-Omer. The Headquarters of Sir John French, Commander-in-Chief of the British Expeditionary Force. On the 24th of September, 1915. Oh, Mum, Dad, I wish I could tell you but I can't: there's going to be a battle! The barrage began three days ago. Day and night. We're going to smash through the German lines, right across Artois and Champagne, all the way to Berlin!

He opens the map.

Enter FRENCH, FIELD MARSHAL SIR DOUGLAS HAIG, MARSHAL JOSEPH JOFFRE – *Commander of the French Army, magnificent white moustaches, paunch – and other British and French high-ranking* OFFICERS *all in immaculate uniforms. They each have a large map, like* JACK'*s.*

FRENCH. Gentlemen, this map shows the present disposition of our six British divisions.

They all open their maps.

JOFFRE. *C'est quoi exactement?*

FRENCH (*terrible grammar and accent*). *Monsieur le Marshal, ici sont notre deposition de notre six divisions maintenent.*

JOFFRE. *Comment?*

FRENCH OFFICER (*French. To* JOFFRE). I think he said this map shows the present positions of the British Divisions.

JOFFRE (*French*). Ah. They have six. We have sixty.

FRENCH OFFICER. They have moved them south, Marshal, to protect our left flank.

JOFFRE (*French*). As I told them they must. They are the junior partner. (*Terrible English.*) Ah. Many thank-yous, John.

FRENCH. *Non, merci à toi,* Joseph.

And now they are all looking at the maps. Some grunts, some shuffles.

JACK (*looking at his map*). No, this can't be right.

JOFFRE. *Ça termine quand, le tir de barrage?*

Incomprehension.

Le barrage, when do he stop?

FRENCH. As agreed the barrage will cease fire at six thirty tomorrow morning.

Incomprehension. An aide takes out a pocketwatch and points to the dial. The French lean in.

HAIG (*to* FRENCH). Hell's bells, Johnny, is it always like this?

FRENCH. Don't worry, Douglas, it can be a bit sticky but we get there.

HAIG. I mean, can't anyone on your staff speak decent frog?

FRENCH. Well, no one on his staff can speak decent English so it levels up.

JACK (*looking at the map*). No. No.

The French have understood.

JOFFRE. *Ah, oui, six heures et demie. C'est bien, nous sommes d'accord. Et le gaz toxique?*

FRENCH. The gas. One for you, Douglas.

HAIG. Yes. Chlorine gas will be released at 5.15 a.m. One hour and fifteen minutes before the end of the barrage. *A cinq et... cinq et cinquante du matin. Si le vent est bien.*

JOFFRE. *Tout à fait. Si le vent est bon. (Angry gesture.)* The Boche. They begin. At Ypres.

FRENCH. I agree. It is a terrible decision. But it was a dirty low-down game for the Boche to launch the filthy stuff at Ypres. Been waiting to get back at the bastards.

JOFFRE. *Nous venger de ces salauds, c'est ça?*

FRENCH. I think we have each other's gist. The ground for the battle this far south is not good, but gas will give us a decisive victory.

JOFFRE. *Si, la victoire!...*

The FRENCH OFFICERS stand dead still, stony-faced as...

FRENCH. Joseph, you may not understand a blind thing I say but with all my heart I wish I could make clear... clear... my sense of gratitude to you and my admiration. It was your brilliance as a commander, and passion as a patriot, halted the German advance on the Marne. Because of you we have beaten them back in Picardy. And now you inspire the great hazard of the attack we are about to launch. We can hope it will not be a bloody affair, but as leaders of men we are not here to be loved. We are here to drive the invader from the beautiful land of France, to lift her from the mud and pain of battles and make her free. And together we will.

JOFFRE *stares at him. Then he goes to* FRENCH *and they embrace emotionally, kissing on the cheek. All applaud them.*

JOFFRE. *Du champagne!*

FRENCH. Tremendous. Champers!

A FRENCH OFFICER *enters with a tray of filled champagne glasses.*

As they are distributed, JACK *tries to attract the attention of an* OFFICER *on the fringe.*

JACK. Brigadier, sir, I must speak to the field marshals…

OFFICER. The hell, Captain!

JACK. It's the disposition of XI Corps…

OFFICER. Get away, the supreme commanders are in conference, know your damn place!

JACK.… Yes, sir.

OFFICER (*aside*). Bloody upstarts. All kinds of riff-raff and lower classes putting on uniforms. Promoting lower orders, could ruin the English class system.

ALL. Victory! / *La victoire!*

Maps are folded up then the French and the British salute each other. They shake hands. Smiles, good humour.

They exit but for JACK.

Scene Eight

Enter a platoon of PRIVATE SOLDIERS. *They are fully loaded with kit.* CORPORAL FERGAL O'HANNAGAN *is with them. They are singing 'Goodbye Dolly Grey', raucously.*

SOLDIERS.
  I have come to say goodbye, Dolly Grey,
  It's no use to ask me why, Dolly Grey
  There's a murmur in the air
  You can hear it everywhere
  It's time to do and dare, Dolly Grey.

  Enter RALPH *in lieutenant's uniform.*

RALPH. And there, suddenly before me, is a captain of men!

JACK. Ralph!

  The platoon begins to sing the next verse.

SOLDIERS.
  So if you hear the sound of feet, Dolly Grey
  Sounding through the village street, Dolly Grey
  It's the tramps of soldiers true
  In their uniforms of blue...

RALPH (*over the singing*). God, this bloody song drives me screaming mad! Corporal!

FERGAL. Yes, sir?

RALPH. Can you please get them to shut up?

FERGAL. Sir. (*To the* SOLDIERS.) Lads, lads! Pipe the fuck down.

PRIVATE. Don't like the choir, Corporal?

FERGAL. You're a lovely bunch o' lasses, see you in Dublin and I'll have you all.

  Laughter. The SOLDIERS *cheerfully slide off their loads from their shoulders and sit against their packs, smoking.*

JACK. God, Ralph.

RALPH. God, Jack.

JACK. You with 1st Brigade?

RALPH. Yes. Terrific lot, new blood coming in all the time though. We're meant to join 19th Division.

JACK. At Givenchy?

RALPH. What's it like up there? Lot of fun?

JACK. It's... (*Hesitates for a moment.*) Lively.

RALPH. Can't wait! You been at the front line?

JACK. No, they keep me stuck here at GHQ.

RALPH. It's all a bit of a rush. The orders have only just come. Feels like we're going into the attack, yes?

JACK. We're entraining your battalion up to forward command. There'll be a march from there.

RALPH. All through the bloody night I do not wonder. Ah well. At least I'll finally get a shot at the Boche.

An awkward silence.

The Ritz seems a million years ago.

JACK. Yes.

RALPH. No hard feelings, Jack.

JACK. No.

RALPH. General staff intelligence officer, me? Leave that to bright buttons like you.

JACK. Not so bright.

RALPH. Come off it, old man. Bet you're having a brilliant time with Johnny French, giving orders to the world.

JACK. It's not like that.

RALPH. Do you still see Penny?

JACK *shakes his head.*

Not after the night of grand passion?

JACK. How did you know we had a night of... a night?

RALPH. All over brigade the next morning. For an intelligence officer you seem to know zilch about yourself.

JACK. I haven't seen her.

RALPH. Well, you're probably well out of it. They say she's changed.

JACK. Changed how?

RALPH. Become a bit of a pants-stealer.

JACK. Pants-stealer?

RALPH. You know, loud.

JACK. Actually, Ralph, I'm not thinking about her, I'm in a bit of a bind, I...

Off: distant whistles are being blown. The SOLDIERS *are at once getting to their feet pulling on their packs.*

RALPH. Hell, they're mustering for the train. Corporal!

FERGAL. Yes, sir, with you, sir! Ladies, please!

RALPH. Open order march, Corporal, no need to bash the blisters.

FERGAL. Open order march! Tip along on your tootsies!

SOLDIERS (*sing*).
Goodbye, Dolly, I must leave you,
Though it breaks my heart to go,
Something tells me I am needed
At the front to fight the foe.
See the boys in blue are marching and I can no longer stay
Hark, I hear the bugle calling, goodbye, Dolly Gray.

RALPH (*over their singing, to* JACK). It's the only song the buggers know!

They are leaving.

Are your mother and father well?

JACK. Yes...

RALPH. Send my regards. One day I really will come to tea.

RALPH joins in with the song, waving his arms cheerfully as they exit.

JACK (*aside*). What's wrong with my luck, why can't I be with them? I'd know what to do!

He remains on stage.

Scene Nine

Enter HAIG and FRENCH and the OFFICER with the champagne, who hovers.

JACK hangs back.

HAIG. You were damnably eloquent.

FRENCH. A tad too Shakespearey?

HAIG. Well, a bit of bull goes down well with the French.

FRENCH gestures to the OFFICER with the champagne, who tops up his glass.

I thought all the champagne vineyards had been shelled?

FRENCH. There are supplies. Can put a crate or two your way if you fancy.

HAIG. Give me a glass of soured milk any time.

FRENCH. Soured what?

HAIG. Milk. Cleanliness within is all.

FRENCH. Turned Puritan, Douglas? Aren't you the man who in South Africa always had a mule freighted for claret?

JACK. Field Marshal, I...

HAIG. Bloody hell, man, step back!

JACK. The reserves! XI Corps, they're…

FRENCH. Captain! Back! Ten paces!

JACK about to speak again but obeys.

JACK. Sir!

He salutes and marches ten paces away.

HAIG. Who is that puppy?

FRENCH. Bright young thing of mine.

HAIG. Temporary gentlemen?

FRENCH. Very much so. Born under a shop counter.

HAIG. That's what they say about me.

FRENCH. The Haig whisky firm is hardly a shop, Douglas.

HAIG. Counts as one, in the eyes of some. (*Looking at* JACK.) Bright, eh?

FRENCH. There's something in him. He tupped Penelope Wedgewood.

HAIG. Did he now.

The two older men look at JACK.

FRENCH (*to* JACK). At ease, Captain.

JACK stands at ease.

HAIG. You said the ground is bad.

FRENCH. It's coal-mining country! Pitheads, slag heaps, rows of little houses, not to mention old shell holes and the wire since the Boche dug in…

HAIG. But you said 'bad ground' in front of Joffre!

FRENCH. Joffre didn't understand a blind word I said. So what matter?

HAIG. The 'matter', John? The 'matter' is putting up a good show all round before the French.

FRENCH. You think I'm not putting up a good show?

A stare.

Douglas, what is this all about?

HAIG. Do you believe in this attack?

FRENCH. Joffre wants it.

HAIG. But do you want it?

FRENCH. I did not at first, nor did you.

HAIG. And now?

FRENCH. Now it is happening. So we win it.

HAIG. But do you believe in it?

FRENCH. For God's sake, man, how can we have this conversation, we're seventy-two hours into an artillery barrage!

HAIG. Whatever our first doubts were, we must be in this with heart and soul.

FRENCH. Well... All I want is us to be 'in this' with shells that actually explode.

HAIG. John! If we are not committed heart and soul, He will not look down upon us kindly.

FRENCH. Who is this 'he'?

HAIG. The Lord of Battles.

FRENCH. Lord Kitchener?

HAIG. The Lord Jesus Christ!

FRENCH. Ah. Faith.

HAIG. I pray you have it, John.

FRENCH. Oh, absolute faith. In gas.

They are staring at each other.

The ground around Loos is bad, we both know it. But the gas, if lavishly used, it will be effective for up to two miles. And in many places, if not along the whole line.

HAIG. You sound like you're still trying to convince yourself.

FRENCH. As Commander-in-Chief it is my duty to convince myself. If the wind favours us the gas will win the day, and our losses will be light. Now I must go up to the line. I am setting up a forward command post at Lilliers, report to me there.

FRENCH *turns away*.

HAIG. One other thing.

FRENCH (*irritated*). What, what?

HAIG (*calls to* JACK). Captain.

JACK. Yes, sir!

HAIG. Come here!

JACK. Yes, sir!

JACK *marches smartly to them and stands at attention*.

HAIG. Clever little bugger, are you, Captain?

JACK. No, sir.

HAIG. What?

JACK. Yes, sir.

HAIG. So what are you?

JACK. Clever little bugger, sir.

FRENCH. Captain Twigg here is on my staff and therefore under my command.

HAIG. Getting uppity though. What you uppity about, Captain? Something about XI Corps?

JACK *hesitates*.

Come come come, boy, this is your big moment.

JACK (*to* FRENCH). Sir?

FRENCH. Yes yes, speak.

JACK opens his map.

JACK. It's about the reserves. XI Corps. They are five miles behind the front line.

FRENCH. So? The 21st and 24th Divisions are Kitchener volunteers. Bloody useless.

JACK. But the Guards Division is with them. Crack troops.

FRENCH. In battle always have a reserve. Now shut up.

HAIG. No, Captain, do not shut up.

JACK. The... The problem is that that far back, they will not be able to follow up the attack. They won't reach the front line before dark.

HAIG. How do you know?

JACK. Because I've walked it, sir.

HAIG. Ha! A hit, a palpable hit.

JACK. The first wave won't have support. The Boche will counter-attack and they'll be isolated. The reserves won't be able to reach them, they will be too far back and with the bad ground...

FRENCH. You damn little tyke, get out of my sight!

JACK. Yes, sir!

JACK salutes and marches off. He breaks.

(*Aside.*) It's so bloody unfair. Why can't they see it... the streaming-forward of the attack, the reserves a second wave to crash forward, carrying all before them, up and over the German lines and across Flanders, even on to Berlin, it should be... beautiful. Oh God, I've wrecked my army career.

He stays at the back of the stage.

HAIG. The tyke is right.

FRENCH. I will not bear this! I will not bear it!

HAIG. Put XI Corps under my command.

FRENCH. No, damn you.

HAIG. Put them under my command and I will march them
forward overnight.

FRENCH. I said no. And it seems I have to remind you that I
am your supreme commander.

HAIG. Yes, so you are, Field Marshal.

FRENCH. Don't think I don't know of your scheming behind
my back, Douglas. You do have the petty mind of a
shopkeeper. You are dismissed.

Both dead still. Then they salute.

HAIG (*aside*). Friends for twenty-five years. But he can go off
like an exploding soda bottle. And the King wants him out so
what can you do?

He points at FRENCH's *head then exits in a fury.*

FRENCH (*aside*). I've little fear of defeat or disaster in this
battle, but it might be little better, or no better at all, than
previous attempts. And, whatever happens, I know I'll bear
the brunt of it. But in cricket terms: if they want to change the
bowler, let 'em. I know we will have terrific losses of life.
War is a very brutal way of settling differences, the more I see
of it, the more I hate it. And no one will ever believe that that
is what the Commander-in-Chief thought, the day before the
Battle of Loos. (*Calls out.*) Captain Twigg!

JACK *approaches* FRENCH *and salutes.*

(*Aside.*) Should not explain to a snip of a boy. But command
is a friendless thing. (*A beat. To* JACK.) XI Corps is led by
Lieutenant General Sir Richard Haking. Haking is a wild man.
Loyalty to and consideration for his troops is... not one of his
characteristics. If I put his corps close to the assaulting
formations, he will disregard all orders and join the attack at
once. There will be chaos. This is the nightmare of command,
Captain: when you cannot trust those below you. Or above.
You have not heard a word of this.

JACK. No, sir.

FRENCH. And you are dismissed from my staff.

A beat.

JACK. I request a transfer to the front line.

FRENCH. Request denied. You can kick your heels here at GHQ. Then I'll pass you on somewhere.

JACK. Sir, I...

A glare from FRENCH. JACK *salutes.* FRENCH *exits.*

So near and yet so far.

JACK *exits.*

Scene Ten

Enter FERGAL, *crawling. His clothes are torn, his skin is blistered by gas.*

Another platoon enters. They wear capes and anti-gas goggles.

FERGAL. Yes, sir... fuck... breath... fuck... what am I, the only Irishman in the London Irish Rifles and I've gone and lost them... Don't let the Boche run over us all... ah breath, ah breath... yes, sir... lost all my lads, sir, joined up with the Dorsets, then they had a bit of bother with gas, didn't have full gas masks... ah breath ah breath... blew the wrong fucking way, sir... caught all my lads... my lovely lads... sir... sir... Lieutenant sir... Where the fuck, the fuck, the fuck are you...

He collapses as...

Enter PENELOPE, *in a VAD nurse's uniform, with* MEGAN *and* TILLY, *also in VAD uniforms. They run, crouching, across the battlefield to a corner of the stage.*

PENELOPE (*aside*). His name is Fergal O'Hannagan. Doorman at The Savoy Hotel. Volunteered and joined the Queen's

Brigade, the London Regiment, shipped to France April
1915. Numerous actions. Promoted in the field to corporal.
Caught by the British gas blowing back at the Battle of Loos.

FERGAL. You do your... fucking... best...

PENELOPE (*aside*). Also injured in the face, like this...

MEGAN (*aside*). He hears it, for a moment, in the air, it sings.

PENELOPE (*aside*). A fifteen-centimetre-wide, high-explosive
shell, fired two miles behind the German lines, from a heavy
field howitzer. Explodes fifty yards away.

The NURSES *fall on their fronts, slapping the stage.*

And MEGAN *holds up a fragment of metal.*

*Tableau. The three actresses stand and demonstrate to the
audience.*

MEGAN. Casing of the shell.

TILLY. Frags.

MEGAN. Fragments.

TILLY. Shrap.

MEGAN. Shrapnel.

TILLY. Metal.

MEGAN. Three-and-a-half inches by two-and-a-half inches.

TILLY. Red hot.

MEGAN. Infected with streptococci in the mud churned up
with flesh of the dead.

TILLY. Spinning.

MEGAN. Travelling at two hundred miles an hour.

Followed by PENELOPE *and* TILLY, MEGAN *holds up the
piece of metal and runs showing its path through the air
towards* FERGAL. *The others fly in her wake.*

PENELOPE *and* NURSES. Wheeeeeeeeeee...

They reach FERGAL. PENELOPE *holds the piece of metal to his face.*

PENELOPE. And takes half his jaw. And his right cheekbone. And his right eye.

FERGAL *falls forward on his face and is still.*

(*To* MEGAN *and* TILLY.) Girls, come on!

PENELOPE *turns away and carefully inspects one of the corpses, then slowly moves on to another.*

TILLY. What do you want us to do?

PENELOPE (*aside*). New ones, just arrived. Bloody useless. (*To* MEGAN *and* TILLY.) Have you seen dead men?

MEGAN. In hospital back in Blighty, of course! But not...

PENELOPE. They dump corpses out here, so they don't clog up the forward clearing station. But they make mistakes...

MEGAN. Mistakes? You mean? Oh.

PENLEOPE. Find one living and it's gin all round.

They – gingerly – look at the corpses.

MEGAN *and* TILLY. No... No... No... No...

TILLY *comes to* FERGAL.

TILLY. Here! Here!

PENELOPE (*aside*). It hangs on, life.

They rush to him.

MEGAN. His face. Like...

PENELOPE (*calls out*). Stretcher-bearers! (*To* TILLY *and* MEGAN.) Don't go silly girls on me.

TILLY. We won't.

MEGAN. We know facial trauma.

PENELOPE. You've seen this?

TILLY. Yes.

MEGAN. Oh yes.

PENELOPE (*calls*). Stretcher-bearers!

> *Two* STRETCHER-BEARERS *appear*.

> Take this man to the emergency clearing station.

> *The* STRETCHER-BEARERS *look at* FERGAL.

1ST STRETCHER-BEARER. You sure of that, miss?

PENELOPE. You will do all you can to save this man's life!

1ST STRETCHER-BEARER. Oh, for fuck's sake.

2ND STRETCHER-BEARER. You really want to do that, miss?

1ST STRETCHER-BEARER. He's more mud than man.

2ND STRETCHER-BEARER. Mud we are and to mud we will return.

PENELOPE. I want your names and I want your numbers.

2ND STRETCHER-BEARER. All right, all right, sweetheart.

PENELOPE. And don't call me that.

> *They slowly pick* FERGAL *up*.

1ST STRETCHER-BEARER (*aside*). VAD nurses. Great girls.

2ND STRETCHER-BEARER (*aside*). Yer roses of no man's land. But you do get the odd pants-stealer.

1ST STRETCHER-BEARER (*aside*). A loud one.

PENELOPE. Sit him up at the station! Don't lie him down!

TILLY. Yes... (*Aside*.) So he doesn't choke on his blood!

MEGAN. We've got a label. Get the label.

TILLY. Yes. Label.

> *She is pulling at her pocket. She takes out a large luggage label, writing upon it.* MEGAN *looks at* FERGAL's *dog tag*.

MEGAN (*reads the dog tag*). 'O'Hannagan. 1st/14th, London Irish. Number 508769.'

Writes this down in a little notebook.

PENELOPE. What do you think you're doing?

TILLY. Put this label on him. At once. Please.

2ND STRETCHER-BEARER. Lost luggage, is he?

1ST STRETCHER-BEARER. Damaged goods beyond repair, more like.

TILLY. He's to be sent to Queen's Hospital Sidcup.

TILLY *is trying to tie the label onto* FERGAL'*s foot.*

PENELEOPE. What is that?

MEGAN. It's for Mr Gillies.

PENELOPE. Who is Mr Gillies?

2ND STRETCHER-BEARER. Anything else you want put on 'im? Poems? Daisy chains?

PENELOPE. Go! Just go! Get him to clearing! And sit him up when he gets there!

1ST STRETCHER-BEARER. Yes, ma'am.

2ND STRETCHER-BEARER. Yes, ma'am.

PENELOPE. Sit him up so he doesn't choke on his blood!

2ND STRETCHER-BEARER. Yes, ma'am, yes, ma'am.

1ST STRETCHER-BEARER. Three bags full, ma'am.

The STRETCHER-BEARERS *exit running with* FERGAL *on the stretcher.*

PENELOPE. Right! Tell me what that was about.

MEGAN. It's a very new hospital.

TILLY. For wounds to the face.

MEGAN. First it was in Aldershot.

TILLY. That's where we were sent. Then he moved it.

MEGAN. To Queen's at Sidcup.

TILLY. He gave us the labels when we knew we were coming to France.

MEGAN. So he'd get the best, sorry worst, cases.

TILLY. Said he don't like lads going to other hospitals, said they are butchers.

MEGAN. Who did?

TILLY. The surgeon. Mr Harold Gillies.

MEGAN. He does rhinoplasty.

TILLY. Plastic surgery.

A beat.

PENELOPE. Well. Then we'd better get more labels done and given out to everyone. Right. Rest. Come on.

She exits.

MEGAN. You didn't tell her…

TILLY. 'Bout Doctor Scroggy? She'd not understand.

MEGAN. No.

They laugh.

TILLY. How can we laugh, seeing men die?

MEGAN. Because nothing is normal here, even our thoughts, nothing is normal.

TILLY. Oh, I am so tired.

PENELOPE *enters at speed.*

PENELOPE. You two! Time for gin!

They exit.

Scene Eleven

JACK *enters. He has a field telephone – box with a crank,
receiver – under his arm. A wire trails to offstage from the
telephone's box.*

JACK (*aside*). You all know what is going to happen to me, I'm
going to lose my face and when you're in a war... in a way
you do know, you've always known, what's going to happen
to you. Every moment you are alive and you are dead.

*He puts the telephone on the ground, lifts the receiver, turns
the crank. He desperately tries to get through.*

JACK *is downstage. Behind him a curtain reveals a room in
GHQ,* HAIG *and* FRENCH, *maps on the wall,* OFFICERS
*rushing back and forth, repeatedly cranking the phone as the
generals row.*

Hello hello...

HAIG. Release the reserve to my command, now!

FRENCH. I will not!

JACK. Hello hello...

HAIG. God, man, the attack is failing!

FRENCH. Elements of the 1st and 6th have reached the village
of Loos.

HAIG. But they are horribly exposed! They must be reinforced!
Release XI Corps!

JACK. Hello hello!

HAIG. Johnny! I can do it. Trust me.

A moment.

JACK. XI Corps is under your command, tell Haking to
advance.

HAIG. Yes, sir! I will give him his orders personally!

The curtain obscures the generals' scene.

JACK. Hello! Hello!

Nothing. He throws the receiver down.

(*Aside.*) No blame. The telephone lines, laid by the Royal Engineer Signal Service, GHQ to forward HQ to front-line posts, wires over the mud, in and out of trenches... getting shot to bits in the shelling. And five hours later I'm sitting in the dark, staring at a telephone that doesn't work. No blame.

A pause.

Then FRENCH *enters. He all but stumbles, pulls himself together.*

FRENCH. Ah, Jack Twigg.

JACK. Sir!

FRENCH. What's the good of a field telephone this far back?

JACK. The telephones in the château... there was no line to your forward HQ. So I just hoped... this connected to somewhere.

FRENCH. But it didn't.

JACK. No.

FRENCH. Remind me, didn't I dismiss you from my staff?

JACK. Yes, but I...

FRENCH. Hunh. Wanted to do your bit?

JACK. Yes, sir.

A pause.

FRENCH. So what intelligence of the day do you have?

JACK. It's patchy. The London got to the chalk pits in the south of Loos. Midday there was a report that the attack was succeeding. But the 9th Scottish in the centre had difficulty at the Hohenzollern Redoubt... and they got hit badly by German crossfire and our gas blew back on them. By evening all the ground won had been lost.

FRENCH. And the reserves...

JACK. I...

FRENCH. XI Corps arrived in bits and drabs. Exhausted. Too late. As you said they would be, clever Jack Twigg, clever boy soldier. So, tell me. Where are the glorious cavalry charges now? Lances to the fore?

JACK. Sir, I am so sorry.

FRENCH. For what, damn you? You have sorrow for me? For me?

A pause.

JACK. Sir, I respectfully request permission to join the line.

FRENCH *looks at him for a long time.*

FRENCH. Go and be a bloody hero. Permission granted.

FRENCH *exits.*

JACK *still on the stage.*

Scene Twelve

Front line. Assembly trench.

A platoon of PRIVATES *led by* CORPORAL CLANCY. *They are in full kit for an attack.*

They all lie down in a line close together and sleep.

A young soldier, EDWARDS, *hugs a football.*

Enter CLANCY. *He claps his hands.*

CLANCY. C'mon, lads, time to be up and doing.

They wake sluggishly. JACK *pushes along the line of waking men and the corpses.*

JACK (*to* EDWARDS). What are you doing with that?

EDWARDS. It's some idea, this. We're going to kick it across to the German trench. For Blackburn Rovers!

JACK. That is some idea. What's the chance of winning the game?

EDWARDS. The playing will tell.

And EDWARDS *is suddenly shaking.*

JACK. What's your name?

EDWARDS. Ed… Edwards, sir.

JACK. It's all right, Edwards. We're all together in this.

EDWARDS. Sir.

He continues to shake.

CLANCY – *London accent – pushes past the packed men to* JACK.

CLANCY. You the new officer, sir?

JACK. Yes, Corporal, replacing… I think it was…

CLANCY. Lieutenant Byrne, sir.

JACK. How is morale?

A moment.

CLANCY. Morale is excellent, sir.

JACK. And Lieutenant Byrne…

CLANCY. Still out there, sir. From yesterday's push. Hopefully today we'll get him back. What's left of him.

JACK. We will try.

Hatred from CLANCY.

CLANCY (*aside*). Another toff. Time to time it does cross your mind: shoot the bastards in the back of the neck. (*To* JACK.) Not with a Company, sir? If you don't mind me asking, sir, seeing your rank.

JACK. I'm from GHQ. Bit of an improvised show.

CLANCY. First time in the line, sir?

JACK. Don't worry, Corporal, I know what I'm doing.

CLANCY. Good to know that, sir.

JACK. The march up difficult?

CLANCY. Roads were very bad, what with the wounded coming down, the mud.

JACK. You've got the look of a man who's done this before.

CLANCY. I was at Mons. 4th Middlesex.

JACK. The rearguard action at Obourg? Hell of a fight.

CLANCY. You could say that, sir.

JACK. And we'll give them a hell of a fight today.

CLANCY. Yes, sir. (*Aside.*) Not a toff. Temporary gentleman. No need to shoot this one, the Hun'll do the job.

JACK. Time is… (*Looks at watch.*) Five thirty. Order of the day is a thirty-minute barrage before the assault. It should begin…

Dumbshow. The SOLDIERS *cower. Some hold hands to their ears. The actors mouth the lines silently, close to each other's ears. So the audience do not hear.*

Any moment now. Here we go. Give the men breakfast.

CLANCY. *Not come through, sir.*

JACK. *Bread and jam?*

CLANCY. *'Fraid not, sir. There is tea.*

JACK. *There is tea.*

CLANCY (*shouting – still in dumbshow, along the line*). *Tea up!*

SOLDIERS (*shouting along the line*). *Tea up! Tea up!*

Dumbshow routine. Each SOLDIER *produces a tea mug.* CLANCY *produces a canteen. The* SOLDIERS *produce tea mugs.* CLANCY *is about to pour when the barrage stops.*

Then they speak aside.

1ST SOLDIER. You think.

SOLDIERS. Yes. / Yes. / You think: yes. / Yes yes. / Yes. / Yes. / Tes. / Tea. / Tea. / Yes.

2ND SOLDIER. My cat's called, oh God, what's my cat called...

JACK (*aside*). And the barrage stops. Silence. And you hear a sound.

The SOLDIERS *make a quiet buzzing sound.*

A pause, the buzzing continuing.

(*Aside.*) It's the flies feasting on the bodies of the dead.

CLANCY. Tea when we get home, sir.

JACK *takes out his pistol and a whistle.*

JACK (*to* CLANCY. *A whisper*). Bayonets.

CLANCY *whispers to the* SOLDIER *next to him.*

CLANCY. Bayonets.

CLANCY *puts the bayonet on his rifle, the other* SOLDIERS *do the same along the line.*

JACK. And the Boche know you're coming and start firing... And! And! (*Shouts.*) Company will advance!

CORPORAL. Company will advance!

2ND SOLDIER. Tinker! My cat's called Tinker!

JACK *blows his whistle.*

Whistles are blown all over the theatre.

The SOLDIERS, *led by* JACK *holding his pistol high, climb out of the trench.*

JACK (*aside*). Oh God! I love it so!

He is immediately hit in the face by a piece of shrapnel and falls to the stage, face down.

Scene Thirteen

All of the SOLDIERS *are dead still.*

Then the actors arrange the corpse dummies in a row alongside JACK. *And exit.*

SOLDIER/ACTOR (*aside*). British casualties at the Battle of Loos: fifty-nine thousand, two hundred and forty-seven. German casualties: fifty-one thousand, one hundred and ten. More dead than at the Somme one year later.

He exits.

Enter PENELOPE, MEGAN *and* TILLY. *All three are desperately tired.*

MEGAN *and* TILLY *begin to look at the corpses.*

PENELOPE *does not help them. She takes a nip surreptitiously from a small bottle of gin,* MEGAN *and* TILLY *see her do it.*

MEGAN. She's…

TILLY (*shake of the head*). It's what she does.

TILLY *comes to* JACK. *He moves a little.*

TILLY. Here's one.

MEGAN (*calls*). Stretcher-bearers!

TILLY. Label. Oh, I've got them.

TILLY *fumbles for the labels.*

MEGAN. Oh, his…

TILLY. Severe nasal trauma.

MEGAN (*calls*). Stretcher-bearers!

Two STRETCHER-BEARERS *enter.* MEGAN *reads* JACK's *dog tag.*

London Irish. Twigg. Number 732451. Twigg with two 'g's.

TILLY (*writing on the label*). Two 'g's.

PENELOPE (*aside*). We were so tired and there were so many, I didn't realise it was him. I didn't realise it was Jack. And that we were sending him back to fight another war. Doctor Scroggy's War.

End of Act One.

ACT TWO

Scene One

Queen's Hospital, Sidcup.

MR *and* MRS TWIGG *enter. They are very nervous.*

MRS TWIGG. They've got a lovely lawn. Trees and all.

MR TWIGG. They have made it lovely.

MRS TWIGG. Haven't they just. (*A pause.*) Pity about the huts.

MR TWIGG. Well, I think that's where they keep them.

MRS TWIGG. What like…

MR TWIGG. Wards, yes.

A pause.

MRS TWIGG. Haven't seen one.

MR TWIGG. No.

MRS TWIGG. Maybe they keep 'em out of sight.

MR TWIGG. They are still people, Rachael.

MRS TWIGG. Course they are. (*A pause.*) Do you think they have to strap 'em down?

MR TWIGG. How d'you mean?

MRS TWIGG. Strap 'em down to the beds, cos of the pain.

MR TWIGG. I don't know, Rachael, really I don't.

MRS TWIGG. Oh, I hope they don't do that to Jack, do you think they do that?

MR TWIGG. We've got to be strong.

MRS TWIGG. Yes.

MR TWIGG. Strong. For him.

Enter CATHERINE.

CATHERINE. Mr and Mrs Twigg?

MRS TWIGG. Yes, I think so...

CATHERINE. I'm Sister Catherine Black. Major Gillies will come and talk to you shortly.

MRS TWIGG. Major Gillies?

MR TWIGG. We don't want to talk to no stuffed-shirt officer, we want a proper doctor.

CATHERINE. Major Gillies is the chief surgeon here. Queen's is a military hospital, Mr Twigg. Strict military discipline applies.

Enter, running, three patients in women's dresses. One of them is FERGAL. *The other two are* LIEUTENANT HARDY *and* LIEUTENANT JONES. *Their heads are swathed in bandages making them faceless. They are throwing a rugby ball about between them. They are singing/chanting the rugby song, taking lines in turn as they run around the stage.*

PATIENTS IN DRAG (*sing*).
If I were the marrying kind
And thank the Lord I'm not, sir,
The kind of man I would wed
Would be a rugby fullback.
And he'd find touch and I'd find touch
We'd both find touch together,
We'd be all right in the middle of the night
Finding touch together...

They exit running. Offstage they can be heard beginning the next verse.

If I were the marrying kind
Which thank the Lord I'm not, sir,
The kind of man that I would wed
Would be a wing three-quarter...

CATHERINE. Would you please excuse me for one moment.

CATHERINE *exits quickly. The three patients can be heard singing.*

PATIENTS IN DRAG (*off, singing*).
And he'd go hard and I'd go hard,
We'd both go hard together,
We'd be all right in the middle of the night
Going hard together...

MR TWIGG (*over the offstage singing*). Well, they're not strapped down.

MRS TWIGG. No. Why are they wearing dresses?

MR TWIGG. Must be medical reasons.

CATHERINE (*off*). You will stop this at once! There are parents visiting this afternoon!

PATIENTS IN DRAG (*off, mumble*). Yes, sister, sorry, sister.

CATHERINE (*off*). Now all of you, get out of those ridiculous clothes!

CATHERINE *enters.*

Men will be men.

MR TWIGG. Er...

MRS TWIGG. They seem quite cheery.

CATHERINE. Mrs Twigg, the patients in this hospital are very ill. You must be under no illusions.

MRS TWIGG. You talking about Jack?

MR TWIGG. How bad is he?

CATHERINE. You must prepare yourself for a shock.

MRS TWIGG. Shock?

A moment.

CATHERINE. It's best you talk to Major Gillies.

MR TWIGG. No, you said shock, you can't give us a shock by saying shock and leave it.

MRS TWIGG. Tell me it's not his eyes…

Enter GILLIES. *He is dressed in a blue suit with a red tie. Over his shoulder he carries a large oar from an eight rowing boat with Cambridge University colours.*

GILLIES. Ah, young Jack's ma and pa!

He swings around. They duck under the oar.

Sister, please fetch the young man.

CATHERINE. Yes, sir.

She exits.

GILLIES. Forgive the oar. Helps me think.

MRS TWIGG. Have you got a boat?

GILLIES. Did have. Cambridge, Boat Race 1904. Rowed number seven.

MRS TWIGG. Did you win?

GILLIES. You had better bet we did. Four-and-a-half lengths.

MRS TWIGG. What a crying shame.

GILLIES. Really?

MRS TWIGG. Sorry, didn't mean…

MR TWIGG. Jack got into Balliol College.

MRS TWIGG. Scholarship boy.

MR TWIGG. So we're Oxford.

MRS TWIGG. When the Boat Race comes round.

MR TWIGG. Dark blue for ever. Yes, the dark.

GILLIES *looks at them, standing before him, terrified. He slowly puts the oar down on the floor.*

GILLIES. Have you been told about your son's wound?

MR TWIGG. No.

GILLIES. But you do know the kind of wounds we treat in this hospital?

They hesitate.

MR TWIGG. You do faces...

MRS TWIGG. ...So we know he's got something... on his face.

GILLIES. His eyes are fine, Mrs Twigg.

MRS TWIGG. Oh.

GILLIES. I know that's the big fear for parents.

MRS TWIGG. Oh.

GILLIES. Many young men here have lost their sight. But Jack was lucky.

MR TWIGG. Lucky?

GILLIES. Lady Luck is with young Jack all kind of ways, Mr Twigg. The wound had concussed him. He was left for dead outside a dressing station. Fortunately one of my nurses was shopping.

MRS TWIGG. Shopping?

GILLIES. Nurses who have served here at Queen's. I have them look out for lively ones.

MR TWIGG. Lively...?

Enter CATHERINE, *pulling* JACK *in a wheelchair, backwards. She glances at* GILLIES, *he signals 'wait' to her.*

GILLIES. Mr and Mrs Twigg, you must be brave. He dreads this meeting. Dreads it for your sake. Do consider, even now, if you want to do this.

MRS TWIGG. We're not ones to complain. If you don't mind, we'll see him.

She looks at MR TWIGG. *A moment.*

MR TWIGG. Yes.

GILLIES *signals to* CATHERINE.

She turns the wheelchair round and pushes it forward.

JACK *wears pyjamas and a hospital dressing gown. He is hunched, holding his head to one side so they cannot see the extent of his wound.*

Why the wheelchair?

GILLIES. Balance problems, inner ear, it happens, don't worry, old boy, he'll get over that.

MR TWIGG. I don't know if I can...

MRS TWIGG. Look at me, Jack. (*A beat.*) Jack?

MR TWIGG. Old boy?

A pause.

Then JACK *straightens and turns his face to them.*

MR *and* MRS TWIGG *are shocked.* MR TWIGG *sinks to his knees. But* MRS TWIGG *controls herself then slowly reaches out to* JACK. *She is about to touch the side of his face when he breaks.*

JACK. No no no g... go away, no no!

JACK *sobs, a horrible sound.*

CATHERINE. Now, Captain Twigg, let's have no silliness...

JACK. Out out!

MRS TWIGG. It's all right, my dear, I'll touch it, let me touch it...

JACK. Ah ah!

GILLIES *shakes his head at* CATHERINE *who turns* JACK *away.*

MR TWIGG *is still on his hands and knees.*

MR TWIGG (*aside*). You're not looking at a face, it's not a face at all, you're looking in the gates of hell, blood and red and black, and rivers o'spit and smashed-up bone, I can't, I... I...

MRS TWIGG. Roy, it's all right.

GILLIES. Breathe, old man, breathe, one and one, and one and one.

MR TWIGG, *controlling himself*.

(*Aside*.) Breath. Spirit. One word for both in Greek.

MR TWIGG. I'm so sorry.

He gets to his feet.

Let myself go, not manly.

GILLIES. Not at all, my dear fellow, only nerves. Strong tea, four sugars, slug of brandy. Sister Black will put you right.

CATHERINE. Yes, Mr and Mrs Twigg, please...

MRS TWIGG. Mr Gillies, can you, will you...

GILLIES. Can I, will I, give Jack a new face? Yes and yes. But we must listen to nature's friend.

MRS TWIGG. Who's that when he's at home?

GILLIES. Time, Mrs Twigg. Time.

He nods to CATHERINE. *She and the* TWIGGS, *going off.*

MRS TWIGG. How do they... eat?

CATHERINE. Tomato soup and cocoa, we dribble it from teapots.

MRS TWIGG. That won't build them up much...

CATHERINE. Major Gillies is experimenting with egg flip, laced with brandy. He pays for the brandy at his own expense.

MR TWIGG. He's a good man, then.

CATHERINE. He's a great man. Whether he be good or not I have no idea.

They exit. GILLIES *and* JACK *remain on stage.*

Scene Two

GILLIES *and* JACK. JACK *speaks with great difficulty.*

GILLIES. Right-ho, honey, what kind of nose do you want? Something Roman? A conk for an Emperor?

JACK....Wha... What?

GILLIES. I'm asking you what nose you want, old fruit.

JACK. You... ask... me... what... I want?

GILLIES. Well, at the moment you've got no nose at all so if you're going to have a new one, it may as well be something spectacular.

JACK. What... I... want... is... to... die.

GILLIES. Tried that, didn't you. If you couldn't get yourself dead at the Battle of Loos, maybe you never will.

JACK. Give... me... something.

GILLIES. I'll give you a new face.

A pause.

JACK. You... can't.

GILLIES. Can.

JACK (*shakes head slowly*). Can't.

GILLIES. Can.

JACK. Can't.

GILLIES. Can.

JACK. C... Can't!

GILLIES. Keep this up, we'll go on the halls. Do a routine together: 'Have a face, sir!' 'No thank you very much, sir!'

JACK. I... don't... want... to... be... alive.

GILLIES. That's not a great act, dearie. Not going to get many bookings with that.

JACK. You... some... kind... of... idiot?

GILLIES. Idiot? Up to you. Would I be a fool to give you back your life? (*A pause.*) Captain, in this hospital I'm walking on air, we all are, we are improvising, fumbling towards new methods, new results. We are doing things in surgery never tried before. Not just in surgery, in life, we are doing things never tried in life. We are playing God and it is terrifying but I want to give you your mug back. May not be as pretty as it was but back it will be! And not the back end of a bus. Yup!

He picks up the oar and begins to spin it about his head.

Need the oar, old dear, helps me think. Blood vessels always tricky little buggers, but yes. Yes! Face, up, face down, facing it! Want to give it a go?

A pause, the oar spinning.

JACK. I... I... I can't! No!

GILLIES *stops rotating the oar and stands it upright, leaning on it.*

GILLIES. Sleep on it for now, old thing. Do that for me?

JACK. Hunh.

GILLIES. Top man! (*Going, turns back.*) Oh, one thing, Captain Twigg. We don't do glum here. Glum just doesn't work.

Exit GILLIES *with oar.*

JACK *alone.*

JACK (*aside*). The barrage. It's stopped. Shh shh, listen, listen. There's a buzzing. (*Direct to the audience.*) What is it? Tell me, tell me! (*Until he gets the response.*) Yes! Yes! Flies on the dead! Company will advance!

Whistles are blown loudly all around the theatre. JACK *stands quickly, arm raised as if he has a pistol in his hand.*

Oh God I...

He falls to his knees clutching his face.

Enter FERGAL. *He too is in a dressing gown and hospital clothes. His face is injured. He is reading a newspaper, close to his face.*

FERGAL. Hey, fella, need a hand?

JACK. No I'm... fine.

FERGAL. Is it wobbly pins? Gillies says it's a bone in your ear, tiny one. Can make the whole world go arse over tip.

JACK. I said I'm f... fine!

FERGAL. Easy, no offence.

FERGAL *takes a few breaths with difficulty then calms.*

Officer, are you?

JACK. Does... it... matter?

FERGAL. Point taken. Mutilation is a great leveller.

A moment. They are suspicious of each other, unable to relate to each other's faces.

He started on you yet?

JACK. What?

FERGAL. Gillies, has he started on you yet?

JACK. No.

FERGAL. He's done my sausage.

JACK. Your...

FERGAL. My sausage.

JACK. I... don't... know... what you're talking about.

FERGAL. My skin graft. Here, have a peep.

FERGAL *undoes his dressing gown. Opens it. The audience cannot see.* JACK *recoils.*

Something to show the girls, eh?

JACK. It's... dis... gusting...

FERGAL. Disgusting it is but I'll say this for it: it's all me. This is how it works.

He folds the newspaper into quarters and holds it against his side.

He cuts a flap of skin away on my belly. Your surgeons, they're all butchers, just a whole lot more fancy with it. He trims along one side like he's cutting you a nice bit of fillet. He leaves it attached to you, aaaaaand...

Rolling the paper.

...Rolls the flap o' skin up, in go the stiches, and, hey presto, there's your sausage of flesh dangling on you.

JACK. But... How...

FERGAL. How's it get to your face? He walks it up your body.

JACK. What?

FERGAL. When the sausage's healed...

He bends the rolled newspaper up to his chest.

He bends it over, stiches one end to your chest, cuts the other. Waits for that to heal then...

Demonstrates.

Walks it again. Up onto your face, then... Hey bloody presto, skin, for a new mug. And it's all you. Hey...

He is having difficulty with his breath.

JACK. Here...

FERGAL takes his arm.

FERGAL. Hunh.

He takes a few more breaths.

JACK. Gas?

FERGAL. Hunh.

JACK. Where?

FERGAL. Loos.

JACK. You were... at Loos? What part... of the line?

FERGAL. Givenchy. First attack.

JACK (*aside*). Oh, fuck it, I remember him. A mouthy Mick, liked to say he was 'the only Irishman in the Irish rifles'.

They stare at each other.

FERGAL (*aside*). I remember him. A stuck-up little prick of a staff officer.

You were at GHQ, were you not, sir?

JACK. Captain Jack Twigg.

FERGAL. Corporal O'Hannagan. I'd not have known you, sir.

JACK. Well... given the state of us, that's not... fucking... surprising.

A moment. Then they begin to laugh, quietly. It becomes uncontrollable. Then they are weeping.

Then an embarrassment comes over them.

A pause.

FERGAL. The terrible thing that I can't explain, to myself let alone any other... I miss it.

JACK. Yes.

FERGAL. Even the mud and the wet.

JACK. Yes.

FERGAL. Even the stink.

JACK. The guns. Sometimes I think I can hear them.

FERGAL. I think they're in our heads. And always will be.

JACK. I even miss...

He shakes his head.

FERGAL. The bodies.

JACK. We'll never... Never be able... to explain.

FERGAL. And we should not.

A beat.

JACK. I don't miss the lice.

FERGAL. Fucking terrible. Even if you could get your clothes washed, back out of the line, the eggs were in the seams.

JACK. I want to go back.

FERGAL. So do I.

JACK. Let's make a pact.

FERGAL. Pact?

JACK. We'll go back. We'll get well... well enough... and go back in the line.

FERGAL. And get to kill a fucking Kraut at last.

JACK. A pact.

FERGAL. A pact. Permission to dismiss, sir!

JACK. Granted, Corporal!

FERGAL *turns away and walks quickly.* JACK *calls after him.* FERGAL *stops.*

Corporal... Lieutenant Dulwich. Any news of him?

FERGAL. You don't know?

JACK. No. I... haven't wanted to... ask.

FERGAL. He's a hero, sir. Got to the German wire. Spent two days in a shell hole. Pulled an injured Tommy back to the line. And not a scratch on him. Got a field promotion. Sir.

FERGAL *exits.*

JACK (*aside*). Promotion. On the battlefield. I got mine on the ballroom of The Ritz. What's that say about me?

Enter CATHERINE.

It's not fair!

CATHERINE. You mean that you're here and better men are not? No, Captain, not fair at all.

JACK. You don't think so?

CATHERINE. What I think is we live in the best of all possible worlds. So we just have to put up with it.

JACK. You can bloody say that.

CATHERINE. Language, Captain!

JACK. I'm a soldier, even though... I'm... like... This... I'm a soldier so I bloody f... fucking swear!

CATHERINE. That's as it may be, but now it's time for your egg flip.

She wheels him away. JACK *gets out of the wheelchair,* CATHERINE *exits pushing it as...*

Scene Three

...a bugle sounds the 'Last Post'.

...Three beds are wheeled on. LIEUTENANTS HARDY *and* JONES *– bandaged, they were the rugby players – and* JACK *get into bed.*

Enter CATHERINE.

CATHERINE. 'Last Post', gentlemen, lights out, please. And goodnight and God bless.

PATIENTS (*raggedly*). Goodnight, sister.

JONES. Doctor Scroggy doing his rounds, sister?

JONES *and* HARDY *giggle.*

CATHERINE. There is no such person in this hospital called Doctor Scroggy and I'd thank you all very much for not carrying on that ridiculousness. Goodnight!

She exits.

A pause.

JACK. Who is Doctor Scroggy?

HARDY. Don't worry, old man, he'll see you all right.

JACK. Why did sister say he doesn't work here?

JONES. Well... he does and he doesn't.

JACK. But... Gillies does know this doctor?

HARDY. That's a deep question.

JONES. Very deep.

They laugh.

HARDY. Better get some shut-eye.

JONES. Best we do. Won't be any if Scroggy does his rounds.

More giggles.

A pause.

HARDY. Don't snore.

JONES. I never snore.

They fall asleep.

A pause.

JONES *begins to snore.* JACK *moans in his sleep. Whistles blow all around the theatre.* JACK *sits bolt upright. He gets out of bed.*

JACK. Get there! To the wire! I'll be first! German wire!

Enter GILLIES *as* DOCTOR SCROGGY. *Kilt, red wig. He is waving a magnum of champagne.*

FERGAL – *in pantomime doctor's outfit – enters carrying a tray of glasses with straws in them.*

SCROGGY. Right, lads, hands off cocks and salute the jocks!

HARDY. Scroggy!

JONES. Scroggy! Doctor doctor, help me!

SCROGGY. What ails ye, lad?

JONES. I've got this rash on my face, doctor.

SCROGGY. Well, it's a mighty improvement to what it was.

HARDY. Doctor, where's my nose?

SCROGGY. It's run off, laddie.

HARDY. Why's it done that, doctor?

SCROGGY. It's in love with a lass called Rosie Parker.

JONES. That's a terrible joke, doctor.

SCROGGY. There is a war on.

HARDY. Doctor doctor, I've come over all peculiar!

SCROGGY. Fortunately my anaesthetist here, Doctor Fergal
O'Flan of Flippin' Finnegan has a remedy! I prescribe:
champagne and oysters all round.

FERGAL *puts the tray of glasses down on a bed.*

JACK *is still sleepwalking.*

The divine oyster, made by the Almighty for the jawless and
the tongueless, a slither of the flavour of the ocean of
heaven, gentlemen, who's up for a taste?

HARDY. You bet.

JONES. You bet.

FERGAL. Got a walker here. Hey, Captain, wakey wakey!

SCROGGY. Right you are, Doctor Fergal, give these drunks
their medicine and I'll see to this one. And have a wee one
while you're about it.

FERGAL *helps* HARDY *and* JONES *to sip champagne
through straws and drink an oyster. Grunts and moans of
difficulty.*

SCROGGY *and* JACK *to the forestage.*

Hey, laddie, where you going in the middle of the night?

JACK. To the German wire.

SCROGGY. And what are you going to do there?

JACK. Hang on it till… I'm… dead.

SCROGGY. And why would you want to do that?

JACK. Because… it's what I deserve.

SCROGGY. Oh, I think you deserve more than that, laddie. (*As* GILLIES.) Captain Twigg, I'm going to count to three then I want you to wake up. One… two… three.

A moment. Then JACK *is awake.*

JACK. Who the hell are you?

SCROGGY. Archibald Scroggy, spinner of improbabilities and physician of dreams, at your service.

JACK. Are you real?

SCROGGY. I get by. Any requests of a medical nature?

JACK. Give me a mirror.

SCROGGY. Ba-bam how d'ya do! I am your mirror! Give us a grin, give us a kiss to yourself. All right, just a wee look.

JACK looks at him. SCROGGY *staggers.*

Ohhh! Cracking me up. Want to know how you look?

JACK. Yes.

SCROGGY. Like a circus clown who's had his face kicked in by an elephant.

JACK. Oh.

SCROGGY. So, looking on the bright side, you've got no problems at all.

JACK. What if I look on the dark side?

SCROGGY. We don't do that here.

Guzzling and slurping noises from the PATIENTS *as they drink oysters.*

Gillies is a clever fellow, he'll undo the elephant damage.
Then you can run away.

JACK, *being won over.*

JACK. Run away, where? Circus, be a freak?

SCROGGY. Clown! You'd get a few laughs.

JACK. Don't think so, sad clown.

SCROGGY. Sad, funny, same thing. Up we go, down, up again.

JACK. I've got a better idea.

SCROGGY. Slap it to me!

JACK. I go back to the front.

SCROGGY. And what would you do there, son?

JACK. Scare the bloody Hun to death.

SCROGGY. Or make them die giggling.

JACK. Here comes the clown with his laughing gas! G... G...
gas, go on giggle giggle in the mud, wriggle, you fucking
Krauts, die. Die. (*A beat.*) Die.

A beat.

SCROGGY. Laddie, all you've got to do here, is get yourself
sane.

JACK. I am... sane.

SCROGGY. Are you now? Sleepwalking in the ward, crying
about the wire?

JACK. It's not my mind, it's my face that's smashed to bits.

SCROGGY. Gillies can fix your face for you, that's just flesh
and skin and bone. It's mind and soul, boy, mind and soul
needs the healing.

JACK. I'm not going to play this game! Fancy dress, fooling
about! Get me to the front.

SCROGGY. That's nah what we're here for.

JACK. What are you here for then?

SCROGGY. To get you back to life, laddie.

JACK. I don't want to get back to life, I want to get back to war. Just... do what you do, cut me, stitch me, pain, blood, I don't care. Doctor doctor – get me back to the war.

SCROGGY. Well, we'll see about that, Captain, but for now let's have a wee snifty of champagne... chance an oyster...

JACK snatches the wig from GILLIES's head. They stare at each other.

All are shocked.

A pause.

Listen!

JACK. What?

SCROGGY. The dreaded sound, the click of sensible shoes in a hospital corridor! What's that clip clop clip clop mean, O'Flynn?

FERGAL. The medical police!

SCROGGY. Sorry, lads, the midnight dispensary is closed.

JONES. One more snifter.

SCROGGY. Patients, orchestrated snoring – go! That is if you're got a nose. If not, make a general moaning sound. Anaesthetist, flee for your life!

With glasses, remaining empties, SCROGGY and FERGAL exit.

HARDY. Twigg! Get back to bed!

JACK. I don't want to play your stupid game!

JONES. Always one that won't bloody well join in!

HARDY. Twigg!

Enter CATHERINE with nurses MEGAN and TILLY as JACK scampers back into bed.

CATHERINE. What is this?

HARDY. You can snore now.

JONES. I can't just turn it on!

HARDY. So fake it.

Snoring and grunting.

CATHERINE *stands still, looking around.*

A pause.

She looks down and sees an oyster shell. She picks it up and holds it up in front of her.

Exaggerated snoring and grunting.

CATHERINE. Gentlemen, I know there have been shenanigans! Nurses! Clear this mess up.

MEGAN *finds a champagne bottle left by* FERGAL.

MEGAN. Scroggy?

JONES. You finish it.

They giggle.

CATHERINE. Nurse! Sink! Pour!

HARDY (*low*). Boohoo.

JONES (*low*). Boohoo.

MEGAN *and* TILLY *clear up and exit.*

The PATIENTS *sleep.*

CATHERINE *comes forward.*

Enter GILLIES *still dressed as* SCROGGY *though he speaks as himself.*

GILLIES (*aside*). How do you describe mass suffering, what is the word, the appropriate noun? 'Tide' of suffering? 'Well' of suffering? 'Fire' of suffering? 'Sea', 'night', 'fog', 'wall', the 'knife', the 'sword', the 'hammer', yes the hammer of suffering, the endless… pulping of a great steam hammer, forever on the human being, the human… face. Or… the 'pity'? No. Sentimental trash, leave that for bloody poets. (*A beat.*) I know. The 'wrong'! The wrong of mass suffering!

He rips the wig off and throws it down.

CATHERINE *approaches him.*

CATHERINE. You cannot give the men drink.

GILLIES *does not reply, staring at the wig.*

GILLIES. Oh dear me, has someone been getting the blighters pissed?

CATHERINE. This is a military hospital. We have a strict ban on alcohol.

GILLIES. Absolutely right. Can't have them falling over faceless in the flowerbeds.

CATHERINE. You cannot go waltzing round the wards, sloshing out champagne!

GILLIES. A 'waltz' of suffering.

CATHERINE. Major Gillies…

GILLIES. Wrong waltz.

CATHERINE. Major…

GILLIES *as* SCROGGY. It's a conga! A conga, whippee, whippee!

Kicking up his legs, conga-style.

All along a trench, Switzerland to the English Channel! Whippee, all scream together, c'mon, woman, knees up! Eeeee, eeeee…

CATHERINE. Giles, stop this! Stop it now!

He stops.

A pause.

GILLIES. I banned mirrors from this hospital. Easy to see why. I banned alcohol for the same reason, to discourage despair. But these are taking-aways, we must have givings. I want to give them something totally unexpected in a war, in a hospital for the horribly injured. Fun!

CATHERINE. I know.

GILLIES. The medicine of fun.

CATHERINE. Yes. But please, get out of that kilt now.

Scene Four

The Ritz. The band plays.

Enter RALPH, *in a captain's uniform. He carries a football.* [*NB: old style! Brown leather and laces.*] *He bounces it.*

Enter PENELOPE. *She is in an evening gown. She carries a drink and is a little drunk. She does a few turns, bored, then notices* RALPH. *He does not see her.*

PENNY. Ralph. Football in The Ritz, darling?

RALPH. Oh, Penny! Actually I'm here for a bit of a regimental celebration. The ball is the guest of honour.

PENNY. The rituals of the British Army are so strange.

A pause.

RALPH. Long time, no.

PENNY. Seems no time at all to me. Maybe we are dancing in The Ritz for ever and the war and all that's grizzly... (*Wave of the hand.*) It's just an illusion.

RALPH. It's not.

PENNY. No. (*A pause.*) Can I have a kick?

RALPH. I don't think so.

PENNY. Be a sport.

RALPH. No.

PENNY. 'Fraid I'll break a chandelier?

She laughs.

RALPH. It's not funny, Penny. This football was taken to the
front by Private Frank Edwards of the London Irish Rifles.
On the morning of the attack at the Battle of Loos, he went
over the top and kicked the ball toward the German lines,
shouting 'kick off'. He and his comrades got across no man's
land. Private Edwards kicked the ball into the German
trenches. A shout went up of 'goal'!

PENELOPE *(cracks up)*. I'm sorry, I can't... I... oh God...
Sorry.

RALPH. It's not funny.

PENELOPE. No. Of course not.

But she is unable to control herself.

So, was that the score? England one Germany nil?

RALPH. The regiment did break the German line. Got into
Loos. One soldier went into a café. Ordered a *café au lait.*

PENELOPE *(lost in laughter)*. Is there a God? There must be a
God...

RALPH. Will you please stop!

PENELOPE. I'm sorry, I...

She manages to pull herself together.

A pause.

So. What went wrong with the football match?

RALPH. How do you mean?

PENELOPE. The German counter-attack? The next day, when
all the ground won on the first day was lost? And the score
ended up, what, a draw, ten thousand dead on each side?

RALPH. Penny, I don't like your tone.

PENELOPE. Tone? My *tone*? Oh God, you men! You stupid, stupid men!

Both upset. A pause.

Who got it back?

RALPH. What?

PENELOPE. The damn bloody ball, who got it from the German trenches?

RALPH. I did.

She sighs.

PENELOPE. Oh, Ralph. Brought back an injured man too, didn't you.

RALPH. One man.

PENELOPE. Two nights in a shell hole with him, during the German counter-attack. I hear you're getting the DSO.

RALPH. Do you?

She stares at him.

Actually, by the time I got the chap back to the line he was dead. The ball wasn't touched though.

A moment.

PENELOPE. Ralph...

RALPH (*interrupting*). I heard you were nursing in France.

PENELOPE. I was.

RALPH. And you were at Loos?

She shrugs.

We didn't bump into each other.

PENELOPE. As one does bump into people on a battlefield? (*A beat.*) You didn't need a nurse.

RALPH. No, thank God. Are you still with the VADs?

PENELOPE. I gave all that up.

RALPH. So... what are you doing now?

PENELOPE. I'm drinking.

RALPH. Penny...

PENELOPE. I lost my nerve.

RALPH. Not for a moment can I believe that.

PENELOPE. The shakes. The nightmares.

RALPH. Not you.

PENELOPE. Why not? Men at the front lose their nerve all the time.

RALPH. They do not!

PENELOPE. You don't know a single soldier whose nerve has gone to pieces at the front?

RALPH. No.

PENELOPE. You should be a nurse.

RALPH. No thanks!

PENELOPE. Don't like blood and bandages?

RALPH. Not that. I'd miss the fun.

PENELOPE. How can you possibly, possibly say, the trenches are fun?

RALPH. I don't think women understand men.

She turns away.

PENELOPE. Lovely to see you, Ralph.

RALPH. Look, Penny... I've got two more days' leave. I was thinking...

PENELOPE. Oh yes?

She turns back.

RALPH. No. I mean... Jack. Jack Twigg. I'm going down to the Queen's Hospital to see him.

She stares.

You heard about what happened?

She stares.

Look, why don't we go down together?

PENELOPE. No.

RALPH. Old time's sake? Aren't you carrying a torch for our young Jack?

PENELOPE. That's none of your damn business.

RALPH. They do say they can work miracles.

A moment.

PENELOPE. Oh, please. I probably saw him, you see. At the battle, at a clearing station. We had labels to put on soldiers with facial wounds. So when they got back they went to Gillies' hospital. I keep thinking, I...

RALPH. That one of them must have been Jack? (*A pause.*) I'm going down with a bit of a party.

PENELOPE. Old regimental chums?

RALPH. Grander.

PENELOPE. A general?

RALPH. Grander.

PENELOPE. You don't mean...

He smiles.

Both of them?

RALPH. Just her.

PENELOPE. I need another drink.

RALPH. My treat.

He takes her hand and they exit.

Scene Five

Enter MEGAN *and* TILLY *who stand at attention. They are excited.* CATHERINE *follows and inspects them.*

CATHERINE. Don't look at her feet. Don't bob up and down. Eyes on her waist, head lowered a little. Keep the arms straight and...

All three curtsey.

Good. Let's have a look at you.

Finds a fault with TILLY *and fiddles with her uniform.*

Nurse! Like you've been through a hedge backwards. (*To both.*) Now if Her Majesty were to speak to you, and I have not the faintest notion why she should ever do that, you first reply 'Your Majesty' and if, against the wildest of unlikelinesses, she should speak to you again, you reply 'Ma'am'. Got that?

TILLY. Yes, sister.

MEGAN. Yes, sister.

Enter GILLIES *in uniform.*

GILLIES. All dandy and dusted up?

CATHERINE. Yes, Major.

GILLIES. Right, big moment. Must dash back. One thing! She is just another person: arms, legs, kidneys, liver. So relax, dear hearts, it's only your Queen.

He exits at speed.

MEGAN. Oh God.

GILLIES *enters.*

JACK, FERGAL, HARDY *and* JONES *enter after him, all in uniform. They line up a distance away on the stage from the nurses.*

GILLIES. Right! No salute, badges not hats, no bow, handshake only when the royal mitt is offered, don't speak 'less spoken at or to, first say 'Your Majesty', second time around 'Ma'am'.

HARDY. What…

GILLIES. What what?

HARDY. Nothing.

GILLIES *as* SCROGGY. If you're meaning what will she make of your horrible ugly mugs, that's up to the royal lassie herself, no? (*As himself, aside.*) Royal visits are the great engine, flimflam nonsense but grin and bear. King didn't want her to come down. But if she likes what she sees she'll keep the place open.

He exits.

The NURSES *and* PATIENTS *wait in line.*

TILLY *suddenly giggles.* CATHERINE *glares at her.*

Enter FRENCH *and* ARBUTHNOT LANE.

FRENCH. Gillies.

GILLIES. Sir.

FRENCH. I was against her coming down here, you know.

ARBUTHNOT LANE. Don't think she can take it?

FRENCH. Just the hint of an 'oh my', of a wince… news of it will travel in the army like wildfire.

ARBUTHNOT LANE. Good for morale if she pulls it off.

FRENCH. Smoke and mirrors, Bill.

Enter HER MAJESTY QUEEN MARY. *She looks around smiling. Behind her an entourage, amongst them* PENELOPE *and* RALPH.

GILLIES *and* CATHERINE *wait for her to say something.*

QUEEN MARY. It's all very pleasant here, Major. Very airy.

GILLIES. Air is important, Your Majesty.

QUEEN MARY. So how many beds do you have in the hospital?

GILLIES. At the moment we are expanding, Ma'am. With convalescent beds, we hope to have over a thousand.

QUEEN MARY. Goodness, so many with your... special injuries?

GILLIES. It's the nature of trench warfare, Ma'am.

QUEEN MARY. Yes. Well. Quite.

She pauses, collecting herself.

FRENCH. It is. It's a mistake. Don't let her see the men.

ARBUTHNOT LANE. Too late.

GILLIES. Ma'am, members of the nursing staff.

FRENCH. I hope in God's name she's not going to be shown any of the worst cases.

ARBUTHNOT LANE. She is. Gillies insisted.

FRENCH. Fucking hell.

GILLIES *gestures to* CATHERINE *and the two* NURSES *step forward.*

GILLIES. Sister Catherine Black.

CATHERINE *curtseys.*

QUEEN MARY. I am very pleased to be here this afternoon, sister. Thank you for all your good work.

CATHERINE. Thank you, Your Majesty.

GILLIES. And Voluntary Aid Detachment Nurse Megan Jones.

MEGAN *curtseys.*

QUEEN MARY. Good afternoon, nurse.

MEGAN. G... Good afternoon, Ma'am. Your Majesty, Ma'am.

QUEEN MARY (*smiling*). You are very charming, my dear.

MEGAN. Oh thank you, Majesty, Ma'am.

GILLIES. And Voluntary Aid Detachment Nurse Matilda Pace-Parker.

TILLY *curtseys*.

TILLY. Your Majesty.

QUEEN MARY. Oh hello, Tilly.

TILLY. Ma'am.

QUEEN MARY. What a pleasant surprise. And looking so crisp.

TILLY. Thank you, Ma'am.

CATHERINE *looks daggers at* TILLY.

QUEEN MARY. Your mother never thought you'd stick to the nursing.

TILLY. I know she didn't, Ma'am.

QUEEN MARY. Well, good for you. (*To all the* NURSES.) Good for all of you. (*To* GILLIES.) And now, Major Gillies, I would very much like to meet some of the men.

GILLIES. Yes of course, Ma'am, please...

ARBUTHNOT LANE. If she keels over, it's only human.

FRENCH. The British monarchy can't be human. Be a catastrophe if it were.

PENELOPE. Is one of them Jack?

RALPH. I think... Yes.

PENELOPE. Which? I can't tell... (*She does*.) Oh. Oh, dear God.

QUEEN MARY *walks up to the four men and stops*.

QUEEN MARY. Gentlemen.

THE MEN. Your Majesty.

As one they salute, then bow. She walks along the line, then turns to them.

QUEEN MARY. I have a message for you from His Majesty the King.

THE MEN. Yes, Ma'am!

QUEEN MARY. He thanks you with all his heart, for your gallant service to the country and to the Empire.

THE MEN. Thank you, Ma'am!

QUEEN MARY. And I wish to add a message of my own.

And, startling everyone, she leans in close to each one and whispers two sentences to them in a whisper which only they hear.

Their line all but breaks with the emotion.

(*Turns to* GILLIES.) Fine men, Major Gillies. The country will never forget them, nor you, for your great service.

GILLIES. Thank you, Ma'am.

FRENCH (*sotto to* ARBUTHNOT LANE). What do words mean any more?

ARBUTHNOT LANE (*sotto to* FRENCH). Those words mean another hundred beds.

GILLIES. Your Majesty. May the staff and I have the pleasure of offering you tea? And the men have prepared something of an entertainment.

QUEEN MARY. Oh, how amusing. Sister Black, Tilly, and you, Nurse Jones, walk with me. Tell me more of women's work here.

FRENCH. Is that Captain Twigg?

GILLIES. Yes. Stay, Captain.

All move towards the exit.

ARBUTHNOT LANE. Entertainment, Gillies?

GILLIES. Nothing to do with me. Fellow on my staff called Scroggy organised it.

ARBUTHNOT LANE. Don't mess this up, Gillies. Took months to arrange.

GILLIES. We are all at the curls and whims of angels, demons, kings and queens.

ARBUTHNOT LANE. I can't understand a damn word you say sometimes, Gillies.

All exit but for JACK *and* FRENCH *and* PENELOPE.

FRENCH *goes to* JACK.

FRENCH. Good to see you, Jack.

JACK. Very good to see you, sir.

A silence. Both stiff, upright, staring at each other.

FRENCH. I... apologise.

JACK. Sorry, sir?

FRENCH. Damn you, you heard.

JACK. You have nothing to apologise for, sir.

FRENCH. You were right at Loos. The reserves were too far back. They could not support the breakthrough made on the first day.

JACK. Other people were responsible, too, sir.

FRENCH. No. It was all pointless.

JACK. It was not, sir. It was glorious.

FRENCH. You, with your injuries, can say that? (*A beat.*) Well, carry on.

JACK. Yes, sir!

FRENCH *turns away.*

The British cavalry are immortal, sir.

FRENCH. In memory, perhaps. But what war has become... it's beyond me, Jack. I pay what penance I can. I tour hospitals. That is what I do. All I can do.

JACK. You are a great man, sir.

FRENCH *is still for a moment, not looking at him. Then he exits quickly.*

PENELOPE *remains on stage with* JACK.

Scene Six

A distance between them.

A pause.

PENELOPE. What did Her Majesty say to you?

JACK. S'private.

PENELOPE. Oh, come on.

He shakes his head.

A pause.

JACK. Tell me how I look.

PENELOPE. You look... horrendously bloody awful.

JACK. Good, you passed the test.

PENELOPE. What test?

JACK. We try it on people. We ask 'How do I look?' and if they say 'You look just the same' or some such rubbish, we walk away.

PENELOPE. Oh, jolly ho. Do you like doing this?

JACK. Like doing what?

PENELOPE. Trying to shock.

JACK. It passes the time. (*A beat.*) If you're blinded you're better off.

PENELOPE. Oh really? How?

JACK. You can't see you've got a face like a blood-soaked sponge.

PENELOPE. Yes, I can see... blindness could be an advantage.

JACK. Gillies has had all the mirrors in the hospital taken away, but in the end you see yourself. In a window or something. I saw me in a puddle.

PENELOPE. Jack, do you want me to just...

JACK. After rain. Funny how people think being human is all in the face. That we are all face. I think of beautiful people I've known, sweet lips, lovely eyes, and they are absolute bastards.

PENELOPE. Or bitches? Bitches like me?

She turns away.

JACK. No! I didn't… No, please…

PENELOPE. What…

JACK. Oh, Penny…

A pause.

PENELOPE. What else… what more… do they have to do to you?

JACK. Depends. Could be ten operations.

PENELOPE. Ten…

JACK. Or more. I've had five already. He did my jaw first. Out of a spare rib…

Points to his lower chest.

…here. Then he got the sausages going.

PENELOPE. Saus…

JACK. Flaps of skin, rolled up. He walks them from your tummy, your chest, up to your face. So the grafts are from you, you see, you don't reject your own flesh.

Points to his forehead.

This scar's the latest. He got the sausage there, then pulled it down and made this bit of my nose. It's going to be a Julius Caesar job. There's more to do. This hole in my cheek o'course and my lower left eyelid's not right. Gillies is great with eyelids. I am an unfinished work of art.

PENELOPE. That you are.

JACK. Well, visit to the freak show done. Are you going to go now?

PENELOPE. Do you want me to?

JACK *cannot answer.*

I should have said yes. (*A beat.*) I can say yes now. AND... I do. Yes, I'll marry you.

A beat.

JACK. Bollocks.

PENELOPE. What?

JACK. Oh, nursey nursey, give us a kiss!

PENELOPE. Jack!

JACK. Nurse and patient romance? S'all bollocks.

PENELOPE. I don't think that's nice of you.

JACK. 'Not nice'? Oh I see, I've got to be 'nice'. Cos when you're injured you've got to be a saint! So all the girls can say: 'Such a nice chap, so smashed up but so brave, I think I'm falling in love with him.'

PENELOPE. I am, I have. Falling, fallen in love with you. I did, that morning after that night at The Ritz, our night. You desperately pulling your clothes on, all guilt, and flushed, like a boy.

JACK. Don't.

PENELOPE. You never wrote. When you came back on leave, you never tried to find me.

JACK. I heard you were a VAD.

PENELOPE. I've given up nursing.

JACK. Why?

PENELOPE. 'Sprivate.

JACK. Because of me?

PENELOPE. Ha! That is one thing I learnt about the wounded: they think they are the centre of the world.

JACK. We are.

A beat.

PENELOPE. I'm not going to give you up.

JACK. Don't then. (*A beat.*) Please.

> PENELOPE *walks toward him and takes his hand. She leans in to give him a kiss.*

> *He points to a place on his cheek.*

There's a good bit there.

> *He giggles. She giggles.*

> *Then they are serious. She gives him a kiss on his chee*k.

PENELOPE. We can have a new life.

> *They embrace. And…*

> *Revealed: the tea party with* QUEEN MARY, GILLIES, ARBUTHNOT LANE, FRENCH, CATHERINE, MEGAN *and* TILLY. *They all have teacups in their hands.*

> FERGAL, HARDY *and* JONES *appear in drag as before. They sing – it's an Al Jolson hit of 1916.*

FERGAL, HARDY *and* JONES.
You called me baby doll a year ago
You told me I was very nice to know
I soon learnt what love was – I thought I knew
But all I've learnt has only taught me how to love you
You made me think you loved me in return
Don't tell me you were fooling after all
For if you turn away you'll be sorry some day
You left behind a broken doll.

> *A silence, all still.*

> *Then* QUEEN MARY *claps wildly.*

QUEEN MARY. Oh, you have fun, that's so jolly, so jolly!

> *Laughter and applause.*

A curtain over the tea party.

Enter RALPH. *He sees* JACK *and* PENELOPE.

RALPH. Hey there, you two lovebirds!

They giggle. Then run off. RALPH *looks at the audience.*

Enter FERGAL, HARDY *and* JONES, *still in drag but with dresses awry, reavealing uniforms. They sing – ferociously – the parody of the Al Jolson song sung in the trenches – with changes.*

FERGAL, HARDY *and* JONES.
A lady spoke to me the other day;
She told me I was looking bright and gay;
Why aren't you in khaki or navy blue;
Fighting for your country as other men do?
I turned she saw my face and screamed
My dear young lady, you don't understand;
I once took my chance.
I left my nose in France;
I'm one of England's broken dolls.

They laugh and exit running.

RALPH *is alone on the stage, still looking at the audience.*

A pause.

He smears ash on his face and exits.

Scene Seven

Enter JACK, PENELOPE *and* FERGAL. JACK *and* FERGAL *are not in uniform.*

JACK. Killed in action.

PENELOPE. I am so sorry.

A pause.

FERGAL. Sorry, miss, but do you know where exactly on the Somme?

PENELOPE. Does it matter?

FEERGAL. Actually...

JACK. Yes.

PENELOPE. It was the first day. First of July. That's all his parents know. I wanted to come to tell you, I thought you...

JACK. Yes.

FERGAL. Thank you, miss.

PENELOPE. Jack, could I...

JACK *looks at* FERGAL. *He nods and walks away.*

JACK *and* PENELOPE *embrace.*

JACK. If Ralph's family, there's a memorial...

PENELOPE. Yes.

She touches his face.

It's healing. Any idea...?

JACK. Gillies wants me to convalesce for six months before he does anything else.

PENELOPE. So you'll leave the hospital?

JACK. Yes.

PENELOPE. Darling, that's wonderful. (*A beat.*) Listen, Jack. I'm going back to work.

JACK. You miss it, don't you. The dressing stations up near the line.

PENELOPE. Jack...

JACK. We're two of a kind.

He embraces her, they kiss.

PENELOPE. Listen! I'm not going to be a nurse. I'm going to join some women. In the East End. They're against the war.

JACK. Against?...

PENELOPE. It's Sylvia Pankhurst's organisation. Come and help, we can work together...

JACK. But... the suffragettes support the war. Emily Pankhurst makes speeches gung-ho for beating the Boche, for God's sake, women are making guns and shells...

PENELOPE. Sylvia's split with her mother. She thinks the war is wrong. (*A beat.*) So do I.

JACK. Why?

PENELOPE. Why? You can ask me that? Why? (*A pause.*) I thought you'd...

JACK. Thought I'd what? Run away and rat on my country? Go slumming with a bunch of pacifists?

PENELOPE. You can't still...

JACK. Can't still what?

PENELOPE. Believe in it? In all this? After what it's done to your face?

JACK. What's it got to do with my face? Me old clock 'n' dial, I thought you'd begun to like it, isn't it beautiful? I think it's beautiful, say my face is beautiful...

PENELOPE. Jack, this is being cruel, don't be cruel to me...

JACK. My injury is a badge of honour.

PENELOPE. Badge? (*A pause.*) Dear God you want to fight again. In the name of... sanity, pity... why, Jack?

JACK. It's my duty.

They stare at each other.

A pause.

PENELOPE. I don't know what you are.

JACK. I'm not a bloody traitor!

She stares at him for a moment, then turns and exits,
running.

JACK *holds his face in his hands then straightens.*

FERGAL *approaches him.*

FERGAL. Jack, fancy New Brighton?

JACK. Fancy where?

FERGAL. Across the Mersey, build a few sandcastles, a few
pints and kiss me quick.

JACK. No, I don't think so.

FERGAL. Ah come, Jack, all this sorrows-of-the-world stuff,
give it a rest. Have a bit of fun.

JACK. Fun.

FERGAL. We'll look up my ma and da in Liverpool. Stay with
my sister Siobhan though, she's a fine girl, you'd like her,
sofa-and-chair job, she won't mind us coming and going...

JACK. We do this before we go back to France?

A pause.

FERGAL. Ah, now.

JACK. Before we go back, Fergal. That's what we said we'd do.
Go back to France.

FERGAL. I'm not doing that, Jack. When I've seen my folks,
I'm going over to Dublin.

JACK. You said your family's in Liverpool. What's in Dublin?

FERGAL *does not reply.*

We're comrades, Fergal.

FERGAL. As men, I feel we are.

JACK. But you're still in the army, you're still an NCO! What are you saying? You're going to desert?

FERGAL. I'll take a discharge, if they'll give me one. If not...

JACK. This can't be, no, after all we... Loos, the months here, under the knife again and again, all that can't be for nothing.

They look at each other, dead still.

FERGAL. I don't belong in your army, Jack.

JACK. Because of Easter in Dublin?

FERGAL. Easter in Dublin. When you're back in active service, don't get posted to Ireland, Jack.

He exits.

JACK (*aside*). How to be true, to yourself, to what you are? I must be true.

He exits.

Scene Eight

Enter GILLIES *and* MR *and* MRS TWIGG.

GILLIES. Thank you so much for coming down, Mr and Mrs Twigg.

MR TWIGG. We're very grateful you wrote, doctor. Major.

GILLIES. Not for me to say to a man, you know. I don't say, just do, don't think just cut and stitch. That's my war.

Enter JACK.

Ah, yes, all the Twiggs of the tree, ha! I'll leave you.

Exit GILLIES.

MRS TWIGG (*sotto*). Oh dear oh dear.

MR TWIGG. Hello, my son.

JACK. Dad, Mum. Didn't know you were…

MRS TWIGG. We've heard.

JACK. Heard what?

MR TWIGG. That you asked the army to go back to France.
And they said yes.

JACK. Well. Desperate for men, aren't they. Even smashed-up
ones.

MRS TWIGG. Oh, Jack…

MR TWIGG. Why do you want to do it, old boy?

JACK. For England.

MR TWIGG. For England.

JACK. Of course.

MR TWIGG. For England. Not for me, not for your mother, not
for that girl who's willing to go through hell 'n' high water
'n' the ends of the earth for you?

JACK. It's my duty, as an Englishman.

A pause.

MR TWIGG. What's your name?

MRS TWIGG. Roy, please.

MR TWIGG. What's your name?

JACK. What do you mean?

MR TWIGG. I asked you, what's your name?

MRS TWIGG. Roy, no.

MR TWIGG. You jumped-up, patriotic parroting, flag-waving
little shit! What's your name?

JACK, *shocked.*

JACK. Twigg.

MR TWIGG. Twigg.

JACK. Twigg with two 'g's.

MR TWIGG. Yeah, your grandpa put on an extra 'g' when he changed it.

MRS TWIGG. Oh dear. Oh dear.

MR TWIGG. The German for Twigg is Zweig. And that's your real name.

JACK. What are you talking about?

MRS TWIGG. Your grandpa and grandma on your dad's side. They were German. They changed their name cos of Bismarck.

MR TWIGG. In the 1870s, lots of anti-German feeling.

A beat.

JACK. But that means... at least... I'm half-English...

MRS TWIGG. Actually... No.

JACK. What?

MRS TWIGG. My ma and pa...

JACK. They were called Hill! Grandmama and Grandpop Hill!

MRS TWIGG. Yeah well... Eichelberger means oak... hill.

MR TWIGG. German oak.

JACK. Why are you doing this to me?

MR TWIGG. You can't blame 'em, boy. Difficult country to live in, England.

MRS TWIGG. Lovely, though.

MR TWIGG. But foreign businesses sometimes... Bricks through the windows. Then there are the Masons.

MRS TWIGG. And now the war's here...

MR TWIGG. It's got mad. They're killing dachshunds.

JACK. No, I can feel it, in me, it is me, I'm English...

MRS TWIGG. Don't get us wrong. When you joined up we was so proud.

MR TWIGG. Always been proud of you, son...

MRS TWIGG. Half proud, but half full o' fear.

MR TWIGG. Now the fear is all there is.

MRS TWIGG. It's not your fight, dear, not really. We are your fight, your family.

A silence.

JACK. Do you know... what job men with wounds of the face get most? Cinema projectionist. So you can go to work in the dark. And sit where no one sees you. Behind the light. (*A beat.*) That's not for me.

MR TWIGG. Jack...

JACK. No. Go away.

MRS TWIGG. Oh, Jack.

They exit slowly.

JACK *alone for a moment.*

GILLIES *as* SCROGGY *runs onto the stage. He carries a magnum of champagne and has a bag of golf clubs over his shoulder.*

SCROGGY. Off to bag some Krauts, are you then, laddie?

JACK. That's right, Scroggy!

SCROGGY. Good man. What will you do with them?

JACK. What?

SCROGGY. The game you bag from Prussia, Saxony, Rhineland, the forests of the Harz mountains? Pheasant are out of season but Boche are in!

JACK. Yes. Yes, I'll go hunting.

SCROGGY. Cannibal, are you then, laddie!

JACK. You bet!

SCROGGY. A feast of Krauts.

JACK. Yes...

SCROGGY. Hang 'em up, let 'em mature, go all gamey, cut 'em up and eat, with a light sauce o'cordite and a side dish o'gangrene, champion portions all round! History is the banquet of the conqueror.

A moment. SCROGGY *crouched, eyes gleaming.* JACK *is wary.*

JACK. Look, the others find you funny, Scroggy, I'll tell them you're out and about...

SCROGGY. It's you I want the fun with.

JACK. There's nothing 'fun' about this hospital.

SCROGGY. No no no, it's all fun, laddie. The war? You're in it for fun.

JACK. You can't say that! Not with what happened to me!

SCROGGY. Is it the fear that's the fun, Jack?

JACK. I want to fight for England. That's all.

SCROGGY. Not that simple.

JACK. It is that simple.

SCROGGY. Nah, it's all knotted and twisted within. It's that feeling, deep down somewhere just above your balls, under your gut, just before the whistle goes and the attack, the op, the risk, the fear, that's what you want. That moment. When you feel alive.

JACK. You're our doctor. And you're sicker than we are.

GILLIES *pulls the* SCROGGY *wig from his head.*

GILLIES. I tell you what I'm sick of, Jack. Healing young men's faces and then seeing them smashed to bits all over again.

JACK. Discharge me.

GILLIES. No.

JACK. You know you'll be ordered to. The army need the men. Even if their noses are wonky.

GILLIES. That nose isn't wonky.

JACK. No. It's true Roman. (*A beat.*) Thank you for all you've done for me, doctor.

JACK *exits as* CATHERINE *enters*.

GILLIES. Another one going back.

CATHERINE. So many.

GILLIES. I feel that all my work is for nothing.

CATHERINE. They're brave men.

GILLIES. Yes. (*As* SCROGGY.) Damn them! Damn them! Damn them!

He weeps. CATHERINE *embraces him. He comes out of it*.

Right! Tea!

They exit, CATHERINE *dragging clubs and champagne magnum*.

Scene Nine

As in the scene in Act One, JACK *with a company of men in a trench, about to advance.*

1ST SOLDIER. You think.

SOLDIERS. Yes. / Yes. / You think: yes. / Yes yes. / Yes. / Yes. / Tes. / Tea. / Tea / Yes.

1ST SOLDIER. God, our Captain looks a mess.

2ND SOLDIER. Bloody hero, bloody indestructible.

2ND SOLDIER. My dog's called, oh God, what's my dog called...

JACK (*to a* CORPORAL. *A whisper*). Bayonets.

  CORPORAL *whispers to the soldier next to him.*

CORPORAL. Bayonets.

  The CORPORAL *puts the bayonet on his rifle, the other soldiers do the same along the line.*

JACK (*shouts*). Company will advance!

CORPORAL. Company will advance!

2ND SOLDIER. Rover! My dog's called Rover!

  JACK *blows his whistle.*

  The SOLDIERS, *led by* JACK *holding his pistol high, climb out of the trench.*

JACK (*aside*). Oh God! I...

  End of Play.